IN PRAISE OF *CONTENT STRATEGY AT WORK*

This book will change how you think about building a brand. Margot's in-depth grasp of content strategy outlines a fresh and essential approach for businesses that want to connect with customers in an age when providing value is no longer optional.

David Armano
EVP Global Innovation & Integration, Edelman

Bloomstein vibrantly brings content strategy to life through engaging real-life stories and step-by-step tactical methods. Underscores the value—and ease—of implementing content strategy. An approachable and actionable guide to put content strategy into practice in a way that will improve every communications project.

Drew Davies
Owner of Oxide Design Co. and Design Director of AIGA Design for Democracy

The firecracker wit and über oomph that Bloomstein showcases in her live talks is now available in paperback.

Sarah Cancilla
Content Strategist, Facebook

For years people have been asking the content strategy community to produce more documented case studies. Your wish has been granted! Margot Bloomstein spoke with dozens of professionals who successfully employ content strategy and content to transform their businesses. Content Strategy at Work captures their entertaining and informative accounts, woven in with pointers on when and how to engage the tools of the practice. If you're looking for examples of how it can be done—even with limited resources—you need to add this book to your professional library.

Rachel Lovinger
Associate Content Strategy Director, Razorfish

Margot Bloomstein strips any high-mindedness out of the notion of content strategy and breaks it down into logical, practical, actionable steps to align your content with your business goals. It's still strategic—but in a way that's accessible and makes sense for your business.

Ann Handley
CCO, MarketingProfs and co-author of *Content Rules*

Margot Bloomstein understands what drives meaningful, measurable change: content, and more specifically, having a smart strategy for creating, organizing, delivering, and maximizing the information, experiences, and stuff people look to for intellectual and emotional sustenance. She has written an important and timely book that articulates the need for a content strategy, outlines a thoughtful approach, and makes the necessary connections between content and every other aspect of how an organization functions. This book is a must-read for anyone.

Brian Reich
SVP and Global Editor, Edelman PR and author of *Shift & Reset: Strategies for Addressing Serious Issues in a Connected Society*

CONTENT STRATEGY AT WORK

CONTENT STRATEGY AT WORK

REAL-WORLD STORIES TO STRENGTHEN EVERY INTERACTIVE PROJECT

MARGOT BLOOMSTEIN

WITH A FOREWORD BY
KRISTINA HALVORSON

AMSTERDAM • BOSTON • HEIDELBERG • LONDON
NEW YORK • OXFORD • PARIS • SAN DIEGO
SAN FRANCISCO • SINGAPORE • SYDNEY • TOKYO

Morgan Kaufmann is an imprint of Elsevier

Acquiring Editor: Steve Elliot
Development Editor: David Bevans
Project Manager: Paul Gottehrer
Designer: Eric DeCicco
Cover Designer: Josh Silverman and Vinny Bucchino

Morgan Kaufmann is an imprint of Elsevier
225 Wyman Street, Waltham, MA 02451, USA

Notices
Knowledge and best practice in this field are constantly changing. As new research and experience broaden our understanding, changes in research methods or professional practices may become necessary. Practitioners and researchers must always rely on their own experience and knowledge in evaluating and using any information or methods described herein. In using such information or methods they should be mindful of their own safety and the safety of others, including parties for whom they have a professional responsibility.

To the fullest extent of the law, neither the Publisher nor the authors, contributors, or editors, assume any liability for any injury and/or damage to persons or property as a matter of products liability, negligence or otherwise, or from any use or operation of any methods, products, instructions, or ideas contained in the material herein.

Library of Congress Cataloging-in-Publication Data
Bloomstein, Margot.
  Content strategy at work : real-world stories to strengthen every interactive project / Margot Bloomstein.
    p. cm.
  Includes bibliographical references and index.
  ISBN 978-0-12-391922-9 (alk. paper)
  1. Internet marketing. 2. Branding (Marketing). 3. Information technology–Management. 4. Web site development. 5. Web sites–Design. I. Title.
  HF5415.1265.B575 2012
  658.8'72–dc23

                                                                                    2011051520

British Library Cataloguing-in-Publication Data
A catalogue record for this book is available from the British Library.

ISBN: 978-0-12-391922-9

Printed in China
12 13 14 15 14   10 9 8 7 6 5 4 3 2 1

For information on all MK publications visit our website at www.mkp.com

CONTENTS

FOREWORD

In most organizations, the word "content" immediately inspires anxiety about the stuff that hasn't been updated lately, or docs that are overdue, or the expensive CMS that still hasn't been implemented despite months of delays.

So, as an individual—a lone ranger in the wild, wild West of content—is there anything you can really do to help bring peace and order to the land of chaotic content?

This is a reasonable question, especially if your job description doesn't specifically address it. After all, if you're a designer, you have enough on your plate. Developers are tearing their collective hair out trying to keep up with cross-platform requirements and ever-shifting standards. Marketing managers are juggling multiple websites, social media accounts, and mobile initiatives (while worrying about what new device they'll wake up to tomorrow morning).

And people who work in corporate communications. Public relations. Human resources. Legal departments. Educational institutions. The government. Nonprofit organizations. If you're reading this right now, it's likely you or your colleagues are constantly creating, publishing, aggregating, curating, and—often—abandoning content, somewhere out there on the great wide web.

But no one seems to be sure whose job it is to *care* about the things that make content *good*: Consistency. Quality. Relevance. Readability. This is the content your users want. This is the content that will work hard for your business.

Here's the deal: this content? It's *your* business. No matter what your role is on any project team, there are ways in which you can introduce the powerful principles and tools of content strategy and immediately improve the way content is created and cared for, thereby improving the content itself.

Creating better content isn't rocket science, and it doesn't have to cost an arm and a leg. There are best practices to borrow, brands to watch that get content right, from concept to launch and beyond. In *Content Strategy at Work*, Margot Bloomstein has compiled an unprecedented number of content samples and case studies to demonstrate what goes right when content comes first.

Her straight talk and commonsense insights shed light on the kinds of questions that keep us up at night: How can we *really* put content to work for our business? How can we shift our organization's perspective from content as a commodity to content as a valuable business asset? How can we use content strategy to increase revenues, decrease costs, and improve our users' experiences?

Content Strategy at Work isn't just a new reference guide for killer content. It's ammunition for that next meeting with your boss or project team, the one where you finally stand up and say: "Content matters, content is complex, and we should give it the resources and attention it deserves." Bang this book on the table. Pass it around. You'll be a hero when you can help every member of your project team understand exactly how they can care for content from start to finish . . . no matter what their job description says.

Kristina Halvorson
CEO, Brain Traffic
Author, *Content Strategy for the Web*

THANK YOU

On a good week, I can look back and recognize that I used my time well. I divided it between selling work and doing work, and both learning and teaching. In our industry, it's easy and necessary to focus on selling, doing, and learning, even if "selling" only involves validating ideas with internal pitches. Those activities all drive immediate or future income. But teaching and mentoring? They rarely pay immediate dividends—yet they're vital investments in how we sustain our community.

So we share case studies, give feedback, and present at conferences. I've had the opportunity to lecture undergraduate design students, conduct workshops, and help "content curious" colleagues explore new career paths. These are not acts of altruism; they're investments in our collective economy. I want our industry to nurture new talent and attract eager collaborators who can offer diverse approaches to problem solving.

And I'm incredibly grateful that other people think so too, because they have long shared their time and experience with me:

Rob Achten, David Aponovich, Sally Bagshaw, Tiffani Jones Brown, James Callan, Bobbie Carlton, Vanessa Casavant, Melissa Casburn, Dana Chisnell, Josh Clark, Jeff Cram, Cammie Croft, Jeff Cutler, Todd Dailey, Bruce Demers, Bill DeRouchey, John Eckman, Sarah Gallant, Steve Garfield, R. Stephen Gracey, Katherine Gray, Matt Grocki, Megan Grocki, Tyson Goodridge, Ann Handley, Kristina Halvorson, G. Jason Head, Frederik Heller, Colleen Jones, Nicole Jones, Jonathan Kahn, Erin Kissane, Jon Kolko, John Krukoff, Ahava Leibtag, Rachel Lovinger, Jeffrey MacIntyre, Mary Martinez-Garcia, Hilary Marsh, Karen McGrane, Renee McKechnie, Tamsen McMahon, Courtney Mongell, Sarah Morton, Ken Neil, Graham Nelson, Birch Norton, David Nuscher, Lee Odden, Eduardo Ortiz, Scott Pierce, Diana Railton, Ginny Redish, Jason Robb, Michael Schneider, Erin Scime, Josh Silverman, Samantha Starmer, Krista Stevens, Samantha Snitow, Russ Unger, Corey Vilhauer, Aaron Watkins, Lisa Welchman, Valeska Whitney, Denise Wilton, and Jeffrey Zeldman, thank you for returning an email, meeting for coffee, introducing me to your clients and colleagues, and sharing your expertise and perspectives. Because you are in the trenches, the web is a better place.

The organizers and members of Refresh Boston, regional content strategy and user experience meet-ups across North America, and especially Content Strategy New England, thank you for hosting me at your events over the past few years. I've explored many of the ideas in this book with you, and your feedback and questions have been so helpful.

Rachel Roumeliotis, thank you for initially bringing this book to Morgan Kaufmann; Dave Bevans, thank you for seeing it through with patience, diplomacy, and humor. Paul Gottehrer, thank you for bringing it to life with peerless dedication. My appreciation extends to the entire team at Morgan Kaufmann.

Karen McGrane, Rick Allen, Melissa Casburn, and Tim Frick, my savvy and thoughtful reviewers, thank you for not letting me form this work as a jumble of rhetorical questions. If this writing is any good, the credit is largely yours.

Josh Silverman, thank you for extending your talent, enthusiasm, and unparalleled taste to this work. We advocate for visual and verbal consistency, but it's even better to experience it firsthand. My thanks to the entire extended Schwa family, especially Vinny Bucchino.

Rick Allen, thank you for giving life to this work on the web and ensuring we practice what we preach in a practical, sustainable way.

Carolyn Wood, thank you for your unflagging interest in the wellbeing of my ideas and voice—and often, me. You championed this project with direction, feedback, and faith; thanks for Skyping me off the ledge time and time again.

Kristina Halvorson, thank you for your boisterous enthusiasm, courageous leadership, and generous mentoring, even at 11 o'clock at night.

Chris and Jim, thank you for helping me to prioritize vacation time for writing when it was so tempting just to run off to Kopp's.

Aunt Wendy and Uncle Alan, thank you for the last-minute encouragement and the long-term examples of hard work and creativity. You burn, burn, burn like fabulous yellow roman candles.

Mom and Dad, how can I write my appreciation? I know you'd say Nana would be proud of me, but I know because of your enduring support and encouragement, she'd be immensely proud of you too.

Ringo, thank you for reminding me that no amount of focused writing can generate the same joy as rubbing a puppy belly.

Mike, thank you for the sacrifices of time, sleep, and creativity you make to support—and edit!—all that I do. Your patience and insight, to both me and this work, always astound me. Thank you.

ABOUT THE AUTHOR

Margot Bloomstein (@mbloomstein) is the principal of Appropriate, Inc., a brand and content strategy consultancy based in Boston. She crafts brand-appropriate user experiences to help retailers, universities, and other clients engage their target audiences and project key messages with consistency and clarity through both traditional and social media.

A 10-year industry veteran and participant in the inaugural Content Strategy Consortium, Margot speaks regularly about the evolving challenges for content strategy at events including Confab, SXSW, Web 2.0, and CS Forum. She lives outside Boston with her husband Mike and Ringo, their adorable and talkative white German Shepherd.

CHAPTER 1

HOW CONTENT STRATEGY CAN HELP

OPPORTUNITY VERSUS PRIORITY

Today, more and more brands—and individuals—embrace the role of publisher. Great, right? Content is king, everyone gets a crown, and who doesn't love a good coronation? Organizations that formerly just sold now also teach, inform, connect, and motivate in order to make a friend—and ultimately, make a sale. We share the CEO's latest insights, publicize project ideas for our products, and go on and on about the virtues of the vegetables the chef's preparing tonight.

That's fine, but a few whitepapers or recurring blog posts do not a publisher make. Kristina Halvorson, president of Brain Traffic and savvy patron saint of content strategists everywhere, offers this perspective:

> "The moment you launch a website, you're a *publisher*. The moment you begin a blog, send an email, participate in social media, build a widget, even show up in search engine results . . . you are a publisher."[1]

That's heady stuff. And for millions of brands and the marketing teams and agencies that support them, that's not a bad thing. But with the opportunities of publishing come immense challenges. Don't just write; write *well*. Don't just blog once; maintain a schedule. Don't just launch an app; ensure your content is appropriate for the many contexts and devices through which it may appear. And goodness, don't just curate content by choosing keywords and automating aggregation; hone your perspective on the topic and continually revisit your collection to maintain its relevance.

Kristina continues (breaks are mine):

> "Publishers plan far in advance which content they will create.
> They have established, measurable processes in place.
> They invest in teams of professionals to create and care for content.
> They would never think of starting with design and then cramming content in at the last minute."

[1] *Content Strategy for the Web* (New Riders, 2010).

But would you? Or would your colleagues or clients?

Whether or not you think you—or your client—is in the publishing industry, think of the content a typical marketing department might create, organize, and maintain:

- User reviews for every product or venue
- Top ten lists, created by the brand, their audience, or both
- Blog posts, comments, and responses to those comments
- Education that spans delivery channels: print, digital, and their sales associates and customer service reps
- Email campaigns
- Hosted conversations and virtual seminars
- Location-based guides that take action from the laptop to tablet and phone

Sound familiar, or daunting? Each of these examples comes to life in the coming pages in automotive advertising, curated lists of tea, healthcare institution microsites, higher education content management, and more. In the meantime, welcome to modern-day publishing on the web—in fact, welcome to the modern web itself: it comprises content, appears on multiple devices and contexts, and demands you plan for its creation—and ongoing engagement and maintenance. So what does successful publishing look like? Whose job is it? How do you go beyond sales and brochureware with a multichannel content strategy? Sit back with a cup of coffee—or really, your favorite oolong—to take in the example of Adagio.

ALL THE TEA IN CHINA, ALL THE CONTENT TYPES ON THE WEB

In addition to buying tea, consumers visit Adagio.com to engage with content that explains its origins, provides a quantitative rating, and offers reviews, which appear with rankings and context. After you try that first sip, you can add your feedback, reap "frequent cup points," "like" a favorite flavor, or easily order something entirely different. With so many options for user-generated content, Adagio welcomes its customers to the content creation process as well.

Engagement goes beyond the website, as Adagio's broader integrated web presence includes outposts on Facebook, Twitter, and YouTube. Integration with Steepster, "an online tea community," lets Adagio foster conversation elsewhere while it drives sales back to www.Adagio.com.

Like most web-savvy brands, Adagio doesn't limit its content—or content strategy—to just text-based copy: maps introduce us to tea rooms, video explains the blending process, and music on a community site lets fans download tracks in the "key of tea." Content combines with frequent, brand- and channel-appropriate engagement to drive the conversation. And across channels and content types, messaging is clear and persistent. Consistent, even, as featured tea farmers appear in images on Facebook and in interviews on Adagio.com at the same time.

TOUGH CHOICES REQUIRE SOMETHING STRONGER THAN JUST TEA

With all these options for content, how does Adagio choose? How does it prioritize, create, measure, and maintain its content? After all, web developers— and many accessible, low-cost content management systems—support myriad features, functionality, and content types. *Can do*, they say, and "sure, we can do that" becomes an expensive, all-consuming death sentence.

You want a blog? We can have that running by tomorrow, says your developer.

A plug-in for comments? Easy.

Video interviews with everyone in the company? Bandwidth for EVERYONE!

Add live chat? AWESOME. Access + conversation = instant customer service, right?

With enough budget, anything is possible; even with just a moderate budget, it's easy to add enough *stuff* so as to overwhelm the screen (and your target audience) with options—and many grotesque websites jostle to prove this. It's a death sentence for many brands, and content managers, who suffer the death of a thousand cuts trying to keep up with all that.

If this is you, you need to prioritize. You need to say no. Whether you're raising requests for the blog, the video interviews, the user-generated top ten lists—or if you're fielding those requests—take a breath. Not everything is of equal importance, especially (though not exclusively) when you don't have infinite time, money, talent, availability, and creativity.

In coming chapters, we'll discuss how different organizations prioritize their content initiatives. Some, like AdoptUSKids, mandate internal stakeholders file creative briefs in which they must explain the communication goals and personas their prospective initiatives will serve. If those initiatives are approved, the web team fits them into a high-level editorial calendar. Other organizations, like Oregon Health and Science University, require new initiatives have both a technical owner and business owner responsible for messaging and accountable for content updates throughout the life of the section or site.

Prioritization means holding your work and efforts accountable to a bigger plan, a sort of raison d'être: why this, and why now? Content strategy focuses that plan, adding additional layers of accountability: beyond the brand or employer you serve, how will you meet the needs of your audience?

After all, just because we *can* add a blog or video interview series doesn't mean we should—our audience may not want it, it might not be right for the brand, or it might be wholly improper for the medium or device in which they want that information. And even if we ignore the fold, every homepage only has so much space and primary navigation should only support so many options. But that's where content strategy can help: as it turns out, while many web initiatives balance competing priorities, there are some things we all want.

WHAT IS CONTENT STRATEGY?

File the buzzword bingo card for a moment—ideally, for the duration of this book—and let's examine what content strategy is and what it isn't.

The last section raised a lot of questions. So many possibilities! How do you make smart choices to ensure the content types, tone, and media in an experience support that experience in a way that's appropriate to the brand and useful to its audience?

Easy. *That's* content strategy.

Or at least, that's one definition for this nuanced and multifaceted practice. And that's the main question I posed to the CMOs, creative directors, consultants, project managers, and content strategists I interviewed for this book. When you can implement a host of features and content types, gated in part by budget and in part by politics, how do you choose?

Before we start planning for a fabulous future, let's take a look at our recent history. It shapes the many definitions and facets of content strategy today.

WHERE'S THIS ALL COMING FROM, ANYHOW?

For over a decade, large interactive agencies have employed teams of content strategists. Former copywriters, librarians, and others worked under that title to plan migrations, prescribe structure for help content, and establish a tone for application error messages—along with other tasks focused on organization, marketing, labeling, and maintenance. In collaboration with designers, information architects, user research specialists, project managers, and developers, we helped some of the most forward-thinking big brands, government agencies, and upstart entrepreneurs put a digital face on their products and services.

Developing a definition

In 2009, the IA Summit convened the Content Strategy Consortium to discuss this in more detail. A preconference event organized by Kristina Halvorson and Karen McGrane, the consortium was the first formal external conference to bring practitioners together with the purpose of discussing and defining content strategy. The 20-some invited participants offered first-hand perspective from a variety of venues:

- Large digital agencies including Razorfish, Digitas, and Sapient
- Mid-size agencies including HUGE, Inc. and ISITE Design
- Advertising agencies like Campbell Ewald
- Government agencies including the Federal Reserve
- Corporations such as REI
- The front lines of freelance consulting

Rachel Lovinger was one of the participants. As she writes on Scatter/Gather, Razorfish's blog about content strategy, participants focused on "defining the practice, identifying the processes and tools, building community, and evangelizing."[2] Rachel herself offers a unique perspective. Back in 2007 she wrote one of the seminal articles on content strategy for information architecture journal, *Boxes and Arrows*. In it, she offers this explanation:

> "Content strategy is to copywriting as information architecture is to design."[3]

By way of analogy, Rachel offered one of the first definitions for our practice, though not without contention.

As web design and creative direction have continued to mature from roots in graphic design, among other disciplines, this analogy may not be entirely suitable. We'll discuss this further in Chapters 2 and 3, which are focused on design and information architecture, respectively. But while this analogy offers a context for content strategy, it still doesn't define it in a practical way that's equally appropriate to tweet-worthy tidbits and pitches to prospective clients.

If you can't explain what you do in those contexts, how can you build visibility or bill the big bucks?

---

[2] http://scattergather.razorfish.com/556/2009/03/25/consorting-with-content/
[3] http://www.boxesandarrows.com/view/content-strategy-the

Ann Rockley offers another definition of content strategy, calling it a "plan of action":

> "A repeatable method of identifying all content requirements up front, creating consistently structured content for reuse, managing that content in a definitive source, and assembling content on demand to meet your customers' needs."[4]

Against those precedents, this is the definition that emerged from the Content Strategy Consortium:

> "Content strategy is the practice of planning for the creation, delivery, and governance of useful, usable content."

Stop the presses—in fact, how can they possibly keep running if we don't even *mention* copywriting amidst all that planning? Presses or not, modern news organizations provide a good model for a broader definition of "creation." Content strategy addresses the creation of content, but as those news organizations demonstrate, creation entails aggregation, curation, writing (along with image making, videography, and audio creation), and usually some mix of all three, in an effort to tell compelling stories.

And that's another working definition. In May 2011, Confab brought together over 400 content strategists to learn from each other. Prateek Sarkar, Director of Creative Services at The Walt Disney Company, led a talk with this statement:

> "Content is story. And content strategy is storytelling."

That definition refers to how content strategy plays a role in determining a brand's perspective and guiding its target audience through content assets and the organization of a site, app, or web presence so that they can glean specific knowledge or a prescribed experience. In this model, the content strategist figures out how to best tell the story: what assets are present, what do they need to prescribe, how should they be arranged, and how should they be updated or maintained?

The story of innovation in Disneyland in the mid-1970s centered on Tomorrowland and its star attractions, the Carousel of Progress and Space Mountain. After a decade, the narrative evolved: maintaining the *story* meant shifting attention to assets like the George Lucas and Michael Jackson

---

[4] *Managing Enterprise Content: A Unified Content Strategy* (New Riders, 2002); see also http://www.zendesk.com/blog/content-strategy-and-customer-service-a-talk-with-ann-rockley.

laser-and-space extravaganza *Captain EO*.[5] And that doesn't even begin to touch on the tactical decisions—in visual, verbal, organizational, and broader experience design—that occur within the attractions themselves to uphold the story and the content strategy.

What's the common thread in all these definitions? They've evolved in parallel with the work we are doing, but share this belief: content strategy addresses planning. This is a practice with its eyes on the prize, mind on the goal posts—and an approach for winning the season, not just a single game. To that end, the *strategy* part of content strategy targets planning, not just execution and implementation. It asks why, how, when, and by whom—not just what. Content strategy asks these questions of stakeholders and clients:

- Why are we doing this? What are we hoping to accomplish, change, or encourage?
- How will we measure the success of this initiative and the content in it? What measurements of success or metrics do we need to monitor to know if we are successful?
- How will we ensure the web remains a priority? What do we need to change in resources, staffing, and budgets to maintain the value of communication within and from the organization?
- What are we trying to communicate? What's the hierarchy of that messaging? This isn't *Sophie's Choice*, but when you start prioritizing features on a homepage and allocating budget to your list of features and content needs, get ready to make some tough calls.
- What content types best meet the needs of our target audience and their changing, multiple contexts? What content types best fit the skills of our copywriters? What content types do we already have?
- What contexts are appropriate for the delivery of our content, and how will we translate our information into multiple content types appropriate for different screens, resolutions, locations, and contexts?
- Is existing content still good? Is it still current, relevant, and brand-appropriate for our needs, our users' needs, and the context in which we want to deliver it?
- How will we get more content to bridge the gaps between what we have and what we need? What is the workflow that already supports that, and do we need to refine it?
- How will we make the case for these new content types to other team members who help shape the user experience?

---

[5] When that version of the future stopped upholding the larger story, Disney replaced it with the model of the bumbling home scientist, and built an attraction around their film *Honey, I Shrunk the Kids* in the late 1990s—only to later replace that with the new *Captain EO* tribute attraction after the death of Michael Jackson.

- Who will do this for launch? Who will maintain content on an ongoing basis? Who will train them?
- How will we help people find the answers, definitions, and other information they need? What are the relationships within our content?

Content strategists also determine when we should ask these questions and who should contribute to their answers. As you can imagine, copywriting is one way to *tactically* answer some of these questions. But the questions are big and our solutions have to be broader than just copywriting if we want to get out ahead of the goals and problems we all wrangle.

Consider the relationship between photography and design. In many web initiatives, you may include photography to visually manifest the brand or illustrate key points like the product array or messaging. With some clients, budgets and subject matter, if you're the designer or creative director you may also art direct a photo shoot; in other cases, you may create the images yourself or source stock photography. And some websites won't require photography at all: check out www.hugeinc.com/news, the news page for HUGE that builds a bold look-and-feel through text-as-image. The services page employs clear typographic hierarchy on an unflinching grid to similar effect.

The news and services webpages of interactive agency HUGE.

Continued

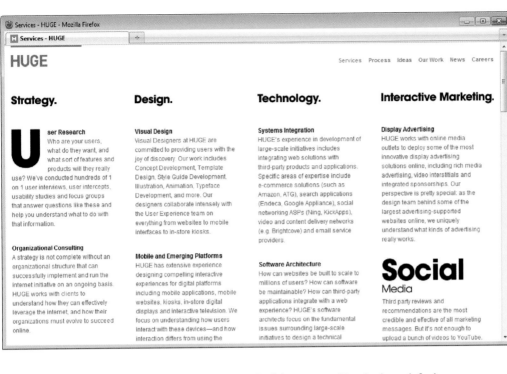

The website for the 2008 Seed Conference also builds a compelling look-and-feel through diction, style, tone, and engaging typography—no other imagery required.

The landing page for the 2008 *Seed Conference.*

In contrast, some web initiatives just don't demand more text. A website overhaul may address the visual look-and-feel while maintaining perfectly good copy. Just as photography is a component of design without being synonymous with it, copy and content strategy have a similar relationship.

WHO SHOULD USE THIS BOOK—AND WHAT YOU CAN EXPECT

Are you a content strategist in an agency or interactive team, marketing department, or consultancy of one?

Marvelous! This book is for you. You'll find talking points, calls to action, and success stories you can share with colleagues and clients to help them buy into what it is you do. Help secure your own budget and organizational support with case studies, anecdotes, and tales from the trenches.

But maybe that's not you . . . yet.

You realize your organization needs to morph into a model of continuous publishing and engagement. And you're on the sidelines; you want to shift your focus away from just copywriting to a broader expanse that includes planning and maintaining content. Or perhaps you've always worked in project management and, more and more, you see that content is an expensive problem that you could help address if you had the right tools and direction. If you're among the "content strategy–curious," you're among friends! Do you recognize angst, expense, and inconsistency around broken experiences, and cry out for processes by which to improve them? Cheer up, buttercup. These pages can absorb your tears *and* help you change the world, or at least your organization.

Perhaps you don't call yourself a content strategist because another title fits you quite well. Maybe you're a marketing director, designer, user experience strategist, information architect, social media consultant—and whoever you are, wherever you are, you're a little lonely. You're missing something that could enrich your work and help you work *better*. It's not about delivering design; it's about delivering and maintaining good experiences—and you know content strategy should be a part of that.

Or maybe, baby, you're a fox! Or more accurately, a FOCS, or Friend of Content Strategy. That's the name the content strategy team at Facebook gives to people like you who champion the practice without necessarily taking on the role. This book will give you examples, inspiration, and ideas for how you can continue to advocate for content strategy and bring it into your team. Embrace your role as a FOCS! Because collaboration with a content strategist is about being friends with benefits—benefits like better planning, timely delivery of assets, and more cohesive experiences.

WE ALL WANT THE SAME THINGS BUT CONTENT GETS IN THE WAY

So . . . planning? Minding the budget and timeline? Giving users and clients what they need, all while you foster pride in the work? And maintain the vision? And enjoy ice cream sundaes as a team on a frequent basis?

Who *doesn't* want these things? (Lactose-intolerant people: I know, I know, sorry about the sundaes.) Across the interactive spectrum, we all want this. So what breaks down? Start with communication, collaboration, and expectations.

Some organizations confuse "copy" with "content," and fail to address the larger matrix of content types they could use to communicate. When copy evolves without a content strategy, it often shows up late, or just for launch, without a plan for ongoing maintenance and sustainable growth. If copy evolves in a silo separate from the visual and interaction design of a user experience—whether that experience occurs in a website, social media presence, app, brochure, or other print collateral—the copy and design can fail to gel and support a consistent, unified user experience. Bad for the brand, and bad for their target audience. But what did we expect, if the design team and the copywriters weren't working from the same communication goals and themes?

That's just a small window into issues of timing, maintenance, and quality. With all the things we say we want, the lack of content strategy is what keeps getting in the way—whether we recognize that problem and give it that name or not.

So, what can we do about it? Embrace content strategy to address these problems—*your* problems. Web workers of the world, unite! Rather than slogging through vague requirements and conflicting requests, let us move forward, armed with clear direction and the courage of our convictions! Rather than clawing at scope and making budget the stuff of petty competition, let us convene as a united team, on the same side with each other, our target audiences, and our clients, and draw on our unique specialties in the name of a common cause!

In other words, this book is for *you*.

- Are you a designer who has to translate abstract requirements into a concrete style of photography and a color scheme despite conflicting brand attributes?
- As an information architect or user experience designer, do you need to reorganize content, but instead end up weeding through blather that may not even be current or relevant in the new website? Skip ahead to Chapter 3.
- Are you the lucky project manager responsible for launching a new website in four months—but you're not even sure if you'll get the new copy by then? This book is for you . . . as is a fully stocked liquor cabinet!
- Are you an account manager responsible for developing a budget, but you don't know whether you'll need to plan for the design and development of 50 pages or 500 pages? Read on, because no spreadsheet will tell you that.
- Are you a copywriter attempting to take on a range of subject matter experts, changing tone, conflicting messages, and a website shell "that's done—you just need to replace the lorem ipsum?" Let's commiserate in Chapter 4.
- Do you focus on search engine optimization, but your SEO efforts draw scorn for keyword stuffing when you don't get to help shape the content? Try the ideas in Chapter 5 on for size.
- Will you be selecting and implementing a new content management system, but you discuss the CMS—content management system, if you're new to this—with IT rather than Marketing, focusing on technology more than culture? Chapter 6 can help.
- Are you launching a social media campaign or blogging strategy without considering content strategy first? Chapter 7 is for you.

I frequently refer to *consultants* and *clients*. If you're part of an internal team, in most cases you can just translate this to in-house marketing and the people outside your department who—hopefully!—levy both expectations and gratitude.

This book is for people across the interactive industry, no matter where you work, whether you helm the Creative Services department in a large corporation or wear many hats in an eight-person agency. Big consulting, in-house marketing, life as an independent practitioner . . . I've spanned that breadth of experiences myself. In writing this book, I collected more of those examples from the trenches: you'll find stories from consultants, in-house creatives, and freelancers who partner with people on both sides of the fence. Whether you work with clients in the literal sense or help realize the vision of internal clients, this book is for you.

WHAT'S INSIDE

Nothing's more discouraging—or boring—than vague suggestions and yawning, expansive platitudes. Without open conversation and thoughtful reflection, content strategy—and content marketing—can drown in the pithy but vacuous tweets, blog posts, and publications that mire many other domains in the broader interactive industry.

Examples, success stories, and critical case studies can help prevent this. Use this book for motivation, talking points with colleagues in your team or organization, and a resource when you collaborate with clients. I've gathered stories that span the breadth of what we do:

- Project sizes from 3 to 30 people
- Project budgets from $5000 to $500,000 (and above)
- Sexy retail brands and more workhorse transactional experiences
- Brands in a range of industries, including food, finance, outdoor apparel, academia, automotive, healthcare and medicine, broadcast media, nonprofit associations, and government agencies

So no more reading flashy examples and then writing them off, thinking, "Yeah, but they had a gazillion dollars! And who couldn't spin gold from imagery of supermodels?!" Because know who spins gold on a tight budget and incremental timeline? The US Department of Energy, with Energy.gov . . . and clearly, they need to save money, time, and attention to focus on securing nuclear weapons instead.

Nuclear weapons always have a way of ending the "yes, but" discussion, don't they?

You'll find examples that focus primarily on the web, but if you're in an agency or internal marketing department that frequently works in print, you can apply these lessons and examples there as well. After all, print often includes a content component, so content strategy is an appropriate way to scope, plan, and manage those initiatives.

Content strategy also drives many successful application development initiatives, and new opportunities in location-based marketing offer ever-evolving challenges for content strategy, especially for making our content contextually relevant.

Does this book include examples from traditional "waterfall"-style projects? Yes . . . and you'll also find examples from teams adopting more agile methodologies (and, sometimes, formal Agile methodology) and approaches to collaboration. As you probably know, tight budgets and quick turnaround frequently encourage close collaboration and fast iteration. In some corporate cultures, content strategy fits into that process quite well.

FAIL TO PLAN? PLAN TO FAIL *AMONG MONSTERS*

From personal experience, you've probably encountered the problems and pains of life without content strategy. But we still keep making the same mistakes, preserving ineffective processes and inappropriate approaches to workflow. It makes sense: "how we've always done it" is a convenient siren song that drowns out the echoes of agony on past projects. If you're too close to the problem in your own organization, let's take a quick look at examples from other organizations that focused on design, business strategy, and technology—all but content strategy. It is that "unknown" that offers the compelling warning: here be monsters! If elements of their stories sound familiar, it's for a reason. Their mistakes are all too common.

In 2009, Bottomline Technologies relaunched PayMode as Paymode-X after acquiring it from Bank of America and renaming it. As part of Bottomline's electronic invoicing suite, Paymode-X has a new look-and-feel and visual branding, but its website "relaunched" in design only. The content is largely the same. Often, this is the result of a team having limited time—a common issue, because we rarely have all the time and budget we'd like on a project. The problem is this: rather than allocating time between design and content, some teams address only the design. Here's the effect:

- Content undermines what should be a unified and informative experience. The tone of the copy is inconsistent among Bottomline's different products and solutions, many of which it has assembled through acquisition.
- Content and design don't play off each other: in some cases, old copy breaks the template it must now inhabit—or leaves it noticeably empty, creating odd gaps in the density of information.
- Search terms and terminology that previously served customers well now go to dead pages as the taxonomy didn't evolve to keep pace with the changes.
- Sales haven't jumped. Potential customers visit the site to learn about the products from the content, but encounter inconsistencies that belie Bottomline's professional and dependable brand and experience.

What about planning for content management without content strategy? In 2010, Parallel Partner relaunched the company's website in a new CMS. Content management may have been a problem, but *easier* publishing doesn't always make for *better* publishing—or content. When organizations silo content management as a technical problem, and technology solution, rather than acknowledging its cultural components, they attempt to substitute

Two of many visual translations of the Bottomline Technologies product Paymode-X.

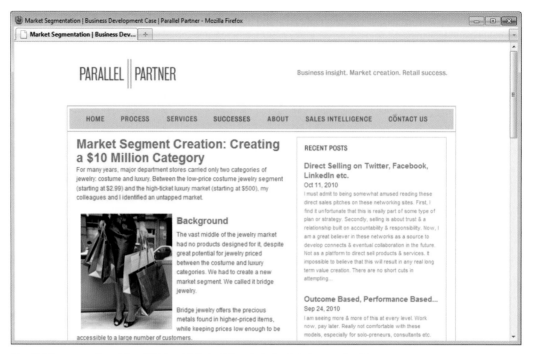

Parallel Partner, a site with a CMS in which the S has little fresh C for ongoing M.

a silver bullet for the hard stuff: time and skill. Without content strategy, the site suffers a couple issues:

- As of September 2011, "recent posts" are nearly a year old. The common culprit? A CMS may offer a "workflow" module, but it needs to reflect the organization's existing content creation culture, otherwise new content will rarely make it to the site.
- The CMS can organize a broad array of content types, but due to conflicting and limited internal resources, the organization doesn't have a way to keep feeding the beast and publishing new content.

Many content management systems treat governance as a technological challenge they can address with a feature set. Lisa Welchman, founder and CEO of Welchman-Pierpoint, describes governance as an organizational challenge instead:

> "Most organizations address low web quality by redesigning their website or installing expensive infrastructure technology. The real reason your website keeps falling into disrepair is because your organization's management practices don't align with the 21st century business dynamic."[6]

---

[6] http://www.slideshare.net/welchmanpierpoint/the-digital-deca-10-management-truths-for-the-web-age-ebook

The business dynamic she describes is one in which the website isn't a project, but an ongoing process. And it's not the purview of the CMS consultant, web manager, or creative director alone. The modern web presence takes a village—a village with time, specialized skills, and a strategy and plan to create and maintain a multichannel experience over time.

So is content strategy the silver bullet?

Be ye not so foolish. Content strategy won't save the web or the experiences we create, but it *will* make them more worth saving—and visiting again and again, on a range of devices, most of which don't even yet exist. What stands in the way of making this dream a sustainable reality? Content. Current, relevant, useful, appropriate content. And if you care about creating good user experiences, this is *your* problem. Whether you are a designer, social media consultant, project manager, CMS consultant, copywriter, or other member of the team, it's time. Time to embrace content strategy to engender the kinds of user experiences you want to create—and that your clients and their users expect.

CHAPTER 2

DESIGNING COHESIVE EXPERIENCES: INTRODUCING CONTENT STRATEGY TO DESIGN

DERIVING DESIGN FROM CONTENT AT MOO

"They could be updated, moved around . . . you could pull out a specific card and stick it on your monitor. The brand guidelines were very much meant to be used—and they were meant for the whole company."[1] That's how Denise Wilton, the former creative director of MOO and moo.com, described the editorial and visual brand guidelines she developed for MOO, the charismatic custom printing company based in the UK.

Is there a place for high-quality paper stock and inexpensive, extremely small print runs in the $100 billion global print industry? As the custom printing industry has commoditized low-cost, low-volume solutions—100 business cards for less than $50? No problem!—MOO stands out for its cheeky, can-do value proposition. How? While its products offer value with fairly quick turnaround, they're often not the cheapest or fastest solution for the target audience, many of whom are freelancers who demand quick turnaround. Instead, MOO maintains its brand through peerless consistency and builds an enthusiastic following by ensuring the brand comes through in every touchpoint and interaction:

- Category nomenclature
- Gallery of audience submissions
- Calls to action
- Error messages, 404-page design, and metacontent
- Confirmation emails
- Product packaging design, inserts, and promo codes
- Tweets from @overheardatMOO

Spanning verbal and visual style and tone, those are just a sample of MOO's touchpoints.

Call it loyalty, call it love, but many of MOO's customers greet even the most mundane interactions, like confirmation emails, with glee, forwarding

---

[1] Wilton, D. (12 April 2011). Personal interview.

them to friends and tweeting out quotes. Naturally, this free advertising only further bolsters the brand and company. Printing millions of cards every month and shipping to customers in more than 180 countries, MOO soon noticed more than half its customers lived across the pond. MOO responded by opening a US production facility in 2009 to meet the volume of orders coming from the US. The headquarters remain in London, and the voice remains distinctly British.

Brand loyalists are "in" on maintaining the magic of MOO. What's the secret? They engage with a brand that never breaks character—ever. This all comes down to how the content and visual design (along with interaction affordances and features) all work together to maintain a cohesive voice and consistently manifest the same communication goals, or message architecture.

A message architecture is a hierarchy of communication goals; as a hierarchy, they're attributes that appear in order of priority, typically in an outline. I usually focus on establishing three to five main communication goals, or big buckets of terms, and define them in as much detail as is necessary for the team that will use the document. In this chapter, we'll discuss how visual designers and content strategists (and, later, copywriters) can apply a message architecture to develop a cohesive, consistent user experience.

In many teams, interaction designers and information architects also use the message architecture for cues to how they should organize and label sections or choose appropriate design patterns. SEO specialists also use it to ensure keyword recommendations reflect the brand personality, as you'll see in Chapter 5.

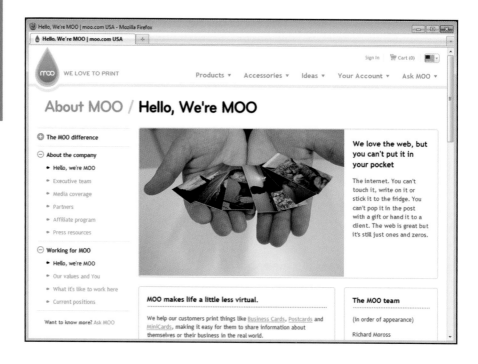

Psst... StickerBooks are stateside
http://www.moo.com/blog

about 10 hours ago via web
Retweeted by 4 people

↩ Reply ↯ Retweet

 overheardatmoo
Overheardatmoo

*Moo.com, @overheardatMOO, and MOO's packaging all manifest the same
communication goals: message architecture at work!*

Notice how the brand is simultaneously both empowering and responsive.
MOO upholds these attributes consistently through a variety of tactics:

- Copy speaks in the first person and conversational sentence structures
- Imagery doesn't just show product, but people interacting with the product
- Emails and the website flaunt examples of customer work
- Copy in packaging and packing slips shares in the enthusiasm of getting new
  business cards

The creative direction in large part stems from the content itself, which has
matured and grown into a more formal content strategy. Denise explained
that the early impetus for MOO's creative direction came from a staple of its
communication, the order confirmation email.

A confirmation email has few tasks to fulfill: tell the recipient that the company received their order, inform them as to what will happen next, and remind them not to reply to that account as it is likely an automated email. MOO takes this mundane, utilitarian communiqué a few steps further by seizing the opportunity intrinsic to unbranded content. This is the body of their order confirmation email (personal communication, 1 March 2010):

```
From: Little MOO | Print Robot <noreply@moo.com>

Hello

I'm Little MOO—the bit of software that will be
managing your order with moo.com. It will shortly be
sent to Big MOO, our print machine who will print it
for you in the next few days. I'll let you know when
it's done and on its way to you.

You can track and manage your order from the accounts
section at https://www.secure.moo.com/account.

Remember, I'm just a bit of software. So, if you
have any questions regarding your order please
first read our Frequently Asked Questions at http://
www.moo.com/help/ and if you're still not sure,
contact customer service (who are real people) at
https://www.secure.moo.com/service/.

Thanks,
Little MOO, Print Robot
```

"The email from Little MOO is one of the first touchpoints after you place an order," Denise explained. "Richard Moross [founder and CEO] wrote that. He got fed up with automated emails that were really impersonal and wanted to bring a bit of personality to it. When I started, that was the one thing in place. Everything else came with that in mind." Denise joined when MOO was a startup and she wore multiple hats, extending the brand through design, copywriting, and community management. "For quite a long time, we didn't have a formal process, but as we grew and had other designers coming in, we knew it would be good—for *all* staff members. You want people to code in a certain way, send out emails in a certain way, and since we printed business cards, we documented the brand in that way."

Denise went on to compile a set of business cards that detailed the brand with cues for verbal communication, visual design, and interaction design. "The cards covered history, values, tone of voice, personality, grammar, color breakdowns, how to use the logo, everything," she noted. "On top of that, there were more detailed guides for how to write for MOO and how to interact with the MOO community."

"Each card in the set worked either as a standalone piece of information, or formed part of the larger piece, the idea being that anyone who needed it could pull out a relevant card and stick it to their monitor to guide them. But each card was written as a standalone piece, so it didn't matter if you got them mixed up. If you were a designer, you could pull out the relevant cards, or if you were a writer and just needed some writing guidelines, you could pull out those cards. They could be updated and moved around, and they were meant for the whole company. They were very much meant to be used." We've all encountered the alternative, as had Denise. "Otherwise, what happens with brand guidelines is they get written . . . and just shoved in a drawer."

Consider how MOO's example mirrors the growth, energy, and opportunity in many areas of the web industry. Are you helping to relaunch a company that has gained some traction and visibility, and now needs to realign its brand, print collateral, and web presence with how it sees itself—and how it would like to be seen? Or perhaps you're in-house, managing marketing for a growing company, helping to launch the next product or reach the next round of funding, all the while grimacing over "cobbler's children" remarks? MOO demonstrates how a brand can hone its consistency over time, even after a period of more organic growth, through two key factors that inform both content and design:

- A single message architecture, stemming from the Little MOO confirmation email, drives all tactical components of communication: visual, verbal, and interactive
- One set of brand guidelines applies to the entire company

In this chapter, we'll deconstruct MOO's approach to design and content strategy through the application of a message architecture. It can add to what you may already explore in a creative brief, or fuel communication with your client that other deliverables and activities manage to sidestep. Either way, if you're a designer, creative director, or someone who manages designers, welcome. This chapter's for you.

WHY BRING CONTENT STRATEGY INTO THE TEAM?

In many organizations, new projects are motivated by design—at least on the surface. Agencies know this well: prospective clients cast out RFPs in search of a new look-and-feel or a "user-friendly interface." Internal creative services and marketing departments may get wind of new initiatives:

- We're launching the new product and the team wants something that looks slick and clean, not too cluttered. We want white space, but we need to still include all the current marketing copy.
- Corporate sustainability and social responsibility has been under attack, so we need to put a more caring, committed face on it. And design a template for a blog!
- We're going to start shooting video of employees talking about the culture here, so we need to design a backdrop and intro graphics.
- Everyone thinks we're old and can't react as quickly as the competition. We need to look hip, for both shareholders and recruiting! Use more lime green.
- Everyone thinks we're too risky and a bad investment. We need to look more conservative, for both shareholders and recruiting! Use more dark blue.

These expectations put a lot of demand on you, the designer—especially as they're vague, subjective, contradictory, or hard to quantify. Just as project managers and analytics gurus know if you can't measure it, you can't manage it, you're in a similar quandary: if you can't concretely quantify and define "more conservative," you can't deliver it or know when you've accurately communicated it to mirror the concept imagined by your client—or clients. If you don't know what they really want, how will you know when you've achieved it? "Dark blue" isn't a communication goal.

IF YOU DON'T KNOW WHAT YOU NEED TO COMMUNICATE, HOW WILL YOU KNOW IF YOU SUCCEED?

This is where content strategy can help. Though content includes more than just words, many content strategists focus heavily on verbal communication, at least as a starting point. Use this to your advantage if you're a more visual person. Why? For one, your client likely communicates in words; meet them on their turf. Send out a content strategist as the advance guard, the scout, the one-man recon team, and watch the magic happen. You'll save time, creative energy, and budget, to do what you *really* do best. As Erin Kissane writes, "Language is our primary interface with each other and with the external world."[2] Let's play to our strengths and employ that interface.

Of course, creative briefs can be a step in that direction. They typically attempt to document the purpose and business goals of an initiative, along with technical specifications. Unfortunately, many agencies omit the area in which they could likely have the greatest impact: an initiative's communication goals.

---

[2] *The Elements of Content Strategy (A Book Apart 2011).*

Some larger strategy consultancies address this by asking brand specialists to hone the messaging in more brand-driven experiences, though they often fall down when it comes to articulating brand principles through the information architecture of massive, content-rich websites. On the flip side, many smaller agencies don't have these specialists or design processes to even support thinking like this. In both scenarios, content strategists fit into that void by translating high-level business and brand guidelines into actionable messaging priorities, all while identifying hot-button communication needs and figuring out how to maintain the experience over time.

Your content strategist can start by engaging the client around their communication goals and priorities—and you can't have one without the other if you want to establish a clear value proposition for the brand. Why does prioritization matter? It's rare for initiatives to have a single purpose or stakeholder; that's why "this too!" is the battle cry of so many departments jostling to have their content dominate the homepage, breaking templates with countless content modules.

On the next page, consider the homepage of Stonewall Kitchen, a purveyor of specialty foods produced in Maine and available online, by catalog, and in retail stores. Stonewall is known for its jams and condiments that seem to capture the breeze and bustle of a farmers' market in little jars with seemingly handwritten labels. Buy a jar of Wild Maine Blueberry Jam, and you'll spread rich flavor on tomorrow morning's toast—and buy into a more relaxed, coastal lifestyle set against a backdrop of sun-bleached curtains and whitewashed porches. It's aspirational, but inviting—except if you attempt to do that through the company's website.

StonewallKitchen.com doesn't offer a clear value proposition because there's no evident hierarchy of communication goals, at least not in how the website presents content to its audience. Is it most important to convey the brand's product range? Probably not, because the product navigation appears in a smaller point size and lower contrast than the headline about the monthly giveaway. Is it important to convey the brand's breadth beyond just food? The page title metacontent lists "kitchen accessories, tableware, home and garden décor and accessories," and those characters are valuable real estate—but the design doesn't speak to those goals; none of the rotating images contain "home and garden décor and accessories," and the cooking school only appears far down the page. Is the brand's heritage important? Perhaps. The biggest text on the page reads "Celebrating 20 Years" but unfortunately it's buried more than halfway down the page.

No content strategist? That's okay. Just because I'm saying a content strategist does this doesn't mean that brilliant teammate with the great shoes is the *only* person who can do it. If you can't find someone to fill that role, you can adopt some relevant techniques to add this perspective yourself.

StonewallKitchen.com is crowded with competing features, images, and content, the result of unclear communication goals.

Does Stonewall Kitchen want to be perceived as enduring, experienced, and diverse? Or is it more important for their audience to see them as focused and premium, an inspiring one-stop shop for creating a picket-fence lifestyle with content about entertaining with fresh farmers' market vegetables and jarred jams?

Before talk of new content, one thing would really help StonewallKitchen.com: a clear hierarchy of communication goals. Enter the message architecture, which MOO manifests so well.

HOW DOES MESSAGE ARCHITECTURE DRIVE THE CONTENT AND DESIGN?

Let's look back at MOO to understand how communication goals can inform the content strategy—and therefore, all the tactical decisions of content types, style tone, visual design, typography, color, etc. This is more difficult with Stonewall Kitchen, whose online user experience lacks a consistent personality and evident communication goals. But by looking across all of MOO's channels and touchpoints—the many ways its target audience encounters the brand—we can reverse engineer a message architecture from their work.

As we previously discussed, a message architecture is an outline or hierarchy of communication goals that reflects a common vocabulary. Working backward from the end product, we can envision that it might look like this for MOO:

```
Cheeky
   Witty and fun
   Young without being childish
Customer oriented and responsive
   Approachable, friendly, welcoming
   Championing and empowering
Helpful
   Accessible
```

Note that a message architecture differs from brand values, which speak more to the company's credo than to how it should communicate with its target audience. Ideally, transparency is a virtue, but values and communication goals don't always align—or may not always be relevant to each other. These are some of the qualities that MOO mentions in its brand values:

- Design
- Innovation
- Community
- Excellence

These are the qualities it prizes as an organization. They may inspire employees and even topics on the website, but they don't indicate priority.

On a similar note, message architecture can reflect a mission or vision statement, but it goes beyond either element to offer a strategy that is both *actionable* and *specific to communication*. This is MOO's vision statement: "Great design for everyone."

Again, it's inspiring, but not an actionable directive.

See how the message architecture captures qualities MOO wants to convey, not the points it wants to make in copy or word-for-word phrasing? On the website for a law firm, this is the difference between saying "we're serious and mature" and *communicating* it by using more formal language, a serif typeface, slightly longer sentences, and images of associates in gray suits with traditional tailoring. If the law firm's message architecture includes the communication goal of telegraphing maturity—perhaps captured in a bullet as "mature, wise, unflappable"—those communication goals would drive the firm to adopt features that reflect a measured approach to new technology. A module that pulls in an unfiltered RSS feed doesn't seem savvy and wise; it seems reactive and may make the brand look like it's clawing for relevance with a whiff of modernity.

In addition to prioritization, concrete and shared terminology gives a message architecture its value. That means getting past edicts like "make us look traditional!" when one stakeholder's "traditional" is another's "experienced," or "conservative," or "American." When your client asks for traditional, don't come back at them with a muted color palette; put on your content strategy hat—or send in the content strategist—to keep digging. Why do they want to seem traditional? Is there a bigger challenge? Does the competition paint them as young and untested? The communication goals are in there somewhere.

ESTABLISH A MESSAGE ARCHITECTURE THROUGH CARDSORTING

I typically approach the message architecture in the context of a project kickoff session, whether I'm meeting with an internal team or external client stakeholders. First, I'll probe their vision for the initiative: why this, and why now? What do they envision a successful future to look like, and how is it different from their present experience? Then we'll move into a facilitated exercise. I've honed this cardsorting exercise over the past decade to help my clients establish and prioritize their communication goals. They're the people who do the real work, much like gym members work with a trainer or patients engage a therapist.

Not that consulting and content strategy are anything like psychological counseling. Oh, no.

This exercise encourages tactile engagement with brand attributes: stakeholders are literally picking up adjectives on index cards to reorganize what they feel is most important to communicate. It also helps us identify conflicting priorities; after all, the new blog, website, campaign, or logo can't communicate both modernity and tradition—or can it? These are the other key benefits:

- Engages stakeholders in a tangible, hands-on way
- Encourages debate and conversation ("what do we all mean by 'innovative' anyhow—and is that the same as being 'cutting edge'?")
- Identifies points of disagreement, team politics, and any history of pain points
- Prevents seagulling[3]
- Forces prioritization and tough choices
- Encourages ownership and investment, long after the consultant team has gone away
- Offers stakeholders a sense of accomplishment early in the project
- Minimizes work and action on inaccurate assumptions

Overall, the goal of this activity is achieving consensus and clarity around communication goals, the foundational elements that inform visual design, content strategy, editorial strategy, nomenclature, and architecture.

Tools, materials, and roles

You can conduct this activity over the phone, but you and the team will achieve greater success if you meet face to face and work with actual cards. You'll need a deck of about 150 index cards, labeled with adjectives most applicable to the client's industry—and maybe a few ringers. You'll also need a large table where the stakeholders can all stand around one end, and chairs so that the rest of your team can remain seated.

These are the adjectives I typically use; I've developed this set through experience with clients in a range of diverse industries, including fashion and finance, recycled packaging and waste management, and medical device manufacturers and the PR companies that always seem to go to bat for them. Though every business is unique, their communication needs are often quite common. (Don't tell your client that.) I typically presort this group to filter out the small handful that might be distracting to the client or potentially inflammatory in that context.

---

[3] When a new stakeholder or a previously-MIA CEO suddenly comes in and . . . *expresses* their perspective, changing the project direction when you're almost through the budget and timeline. You know, the old swoop 'n' poop.

- proactive
- trusted
- cool
- narrow
- slick
- value-oriented
- actionable
- tailored
- down-to-earth
- practical
- custom
- innovative
- hip
- conservative
- urban
- customer-oriented
- market-driven
- professional
- technological
- aggressive
- visionary
- white collar

- tactical
- responsive
- consistent
- traditional
- savvy
- eclectic
- broad
- high-quality
- friendly
- fun
- the thought leader
- current
- approachable
- welcoming
- blue collar
- strategic
- premium
- classic
- cutting edge
- reactive
- national
- detail oriented

- timeless
- elegant
- accessible
- responsible
- sexy
- high-level
- bleeding edge
- tried-and-true
- rural
- in touch
- wise
- empowering
- assertive
- informal
- progressive
- modern
- expensive
- authentic
- flexible
- international
- formal
- fair
- trendy

- simple
- casual
- historic
- serious
- regional
- reliable
- efficient
- diverse
- elite
- relationship-oriented
- driven
- leading edge
- experienced
- smart
- focused
- structured
- timely
- community-building
- pioneering
- lavish
- global

Add to this three label cards:

- Who we are
- Who we'd like to be
- Who we're not

Allot 45–60 minutes during the kickoff, depending on the number of participants and their decision-making abilities. In general, the activity works best with no more than six client stakeholders and one facilitator, who may double as note taker. Who's the facilitator? As a content strategist, I usually wear this hat, but anyone can do this. If you wear many hats as a communication-focused designer or creative director, embrace the hat head! Titles are less important than action.

It's important that you involve all the stakeholders in the room—don't let anyone hang back like a shadowy presence, ready to swoop in and derail activities. Instead, involve everyone by engaging the wallflowers and working with the project manager ahead of time to ensure the kickoff schedule brings the main decision makers into the room at this point. If there are other people who will be involved in project execution but who don't have a stake in the project's goals, explore ways to excuse them for this session, because they may be a distraction or derail progress. When people hang back, they may not fully support decisions of the group and may raise concerns after the fact. Conversely, when members of the group mentally check out or excuse themselves to "chime in later" after others have started sorting the cards, they may subconsciously elevate themselves into a position of approval or disapproval.

Remember how we said you need a table with room for the stakeholders to stand, but with chairs so that the other members of your team can remain sitting? That's by design. Beyond the stakeholder participants and facilitator, I prefer to limit interaction from other team members in the room. Intervention can distract or influence the clients' open discussion and debate. Instead, other team members should stay focused, avoid side conversations, but be careful not to hover. Body language matters: while encouraging the stakeholders to stand, as a facilitator, I try to remain sitting during this exercise. By standing up, we can seem overbearing—not ideal when we're trying to encourage discussion in an open manner.

Step one: categorize

If you're the facilitator, kick off the exercise by introducing this approach for gleaning a lot of brand information very quickly. Though your client may have already provided some information on brand values, this is an opportunity to hear it in their own words—also a key point if you're serving an internal "client" at an organization at which you both work. This is their chance to separate communication goals from brand values, so have at it. Mention that you'll document as you go and summarize in the message architecture. Divide the stack of prefiltered cards between the participants or toss them across the table, and explain that they need to divvy them into three categories:

- Who we are: "How do you think your brand is currently perceived?"
- Who we'd like to be: "How would you *like* the brand to be perceived? What are the aspirational qualities you want to own in the hearts and minds of customers,

prospects, and competitors?" Remind them that this initiative—whatever it is—is aspirational, so this is their chance to grow.

- Who we're not: "Which terms don't you want to associate with your brand? Which terms just aren't relevant, or maybe better apply to a competitor?"

Mention that some cards may be ringers and inapplicable to their brand. However, most of the cards will fit into one of the three categories. Make space for the three categories by laying out cards to label them across one end of the table, then let your participants start distributing the remaining cards.

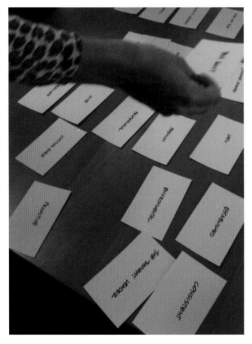

Cardsorting begins with stakeholders categorizing adjectives to describe their brand: who we are, who we're not, and who we'd like to be.

After you explain the directions, step back and tell them to go on gut instinct, get to work—then hush. Your presence may assert false time pressure, and they need to discuss among themselves. This portion of the exercise should take no more than 15 minutes, but the pauses, hesitation, and snap decisions are all worth noting. Jot them down. Do participants seem to giggle or grimace over certain terms? Take note. There's probably a backstory worth discussing—like a project that had similar goals or politically charged lingo. Avoid those minefields by identifying them now.

If participants have questions about any of these categories or the terms, try to push them to come up with their own answers or interpretations—"what do you think it means?" Some terms are intentionally ambiguous to invite discourse. Others, like "cutting edge," "leading edge," and "bleeding edge" may be close in meaning but expose nuance shared by your stakeholders. Let them clue you in on the difference; this is where denotation and connotation come into play.

After 90% of the cards are in categories, if it's getting tough, go ahead and dig into those remaining cards. If they're not ringers, ask the participants how individual cards fit into the developing schema. You may want to point to similar terms that they easily categorized, and capture discussion about why seemingly similar terms didn't work.

Wrap up this step by asking a few questions, both for their answers and how participants answer them. Favor open-ended questions to encourage discussion; here are some examples, some of which use seemingly obvious pairs:

- "I see you have 'traditional' in this column, but not 'conservative.' How come?"
- "Could you tell me more about why you put 'cutting edge' in this category?"

- "What were you thinking when you put 'cutting edge' here, but 'bleeding edge' there?"
- "It seemed like you hesitated when you put 'minimal' in this category. Why?"
- "You put 'strategic' and 'tactical' in the same category. Are they opposites, or are they not really on the same continuum? What was your reasoning there?"

Take note of how participants respond; you'll want to know if their culture perceives a word like "innovative" as trite or overused so that you can avoid it in copywriting down the road. Also capture the unity and consensus.

Some terms will seem like obvious pairs or clear opposites. You may want to ask follow-up questions about these cards, like "Why did you put both 'traditional' and 'modern' in the 'we'd like to be' column? What's that about?"

- bleeding edge vs. cutting edge
- blue collar vs. white collar
- casual vs. formal vs. professional
- cool vs. hip
- friendly vs. aggressive
- global vs. national vs. regional
- hands-on vs. tactical
- assertive vs. aggressive
- tactical vs. strategic
- innovative vs. pioneering
- modern vs. traditional
- premium vs. value-oriented
- savvy vs. smart vs. wise
- strategic vs. tactical

In step two, stakeholders filter and reorganize the cards to focus on how they'd like the brand to be perceived through the work you're doing.

Step two: filter

After digging into their categories for a few minutes, move on to step two for the next 10–15 minutes. Ask the stakeholders what qualities they want to hold on to—figuratively and, for now, literally—as they move forward. What does the company or brand currently do well, and what would they like to be when they grow up? Are there qualities in the future that will trump or subsume present qualities—like if they'd like to be seen as "international" instead of just "national"? Ask them to keep this in mind and move the appropriate cards from the "we are" column to the "we'd like to be" column. You can gather up the cards in the "who we're not" column; we don't need to focus there anymore.

As with the first step, only jump into the process if it seems to be suffering or slowing down. You're there to ensure the exercise moves along, but realize it will also pull itself along at its own pace. Don't belabor this step; after just a few minutes the participants will thin out their "current state" column and will likely have a pretty dense "future state" column.

Step three: prioritize and close

Now focus just on the "we'd like to be" column, and sweep the other cards from the table so that participants can play with proximity and space to explain relationships. Ask the participants to check out what's left on the table. If they're comfortable with what's there, remind them that to do an effective job of communicating, we have to make tough choices about how we focus our attention—after all, that's how their target audience will eventually focus *their* attention. Time to make the tough strategic choices; later, you'll be able to ground tactical choices, like what really deserves homepage real estate, on these decisions.

Not everything can be top priority, so ask them to rank the attributes or groups of attributes. Some natural groups might start to form—maybe a set of cards just refers to how they have to get in the door or their business culture, or how they'd like to be perceived by investors. As these groups start to reveal themselves, have them push those cards together. You may need to take a more active role at this stage to help them see those groups.

After three to six groups emerge and the stakeholders are discussing those clumps, have them loop you in to the conversation. Time to prioritize the goals and then tell you the story of those aspirations. What comes first, and what's the connection with the next group? Take this all down, in either an outline or mind map, and then congratulate the team. They did what you needed them to do: they achieved consensus on and clarity around a concrete hierarchy of communication goals with a vocabulary that they and you understand. What comes next? Explain that you'll go back and synthesize this list into a prioritized message architecture that will be a foundation for all the visual and verbal communication in the project.

QUICK AND DIRTY: ESTABLISH A MESSAGE ARCHITECTURE WITH A VENN DIAGRAM

Another approach to prioritizing communication goals employs a Venn diagram and whiteboard. This method is less hands-on and may not deliver the detail and specificity of cardsorting, but it's valuable for stakeholder

As you well know, all the divisions in the company can't have a spot front and center on the homepage, and not all new products deserve the hero shot on section landing pages. Force your client to prioritize now, when their communication goals are just cards on a table, without ties to departments or industry trends. You'll save time, budget, and effort later on when they have to confront tough decisions. A message architecture can help them—and you—say no, with the confidence that they'll stay true to their own priorities.

teams that may not have the patience or brand subject matter expertise to engage in cardsorting.

Tools, materials, and roles

At a whiteboard showing two large circles in a Venn diagram, arm your stakeholders with several dry-erase markers. As with the brand attributes cardsorting exercise, you'll want one facilitator to do most of the stakeholder engagement, but let your stakeholders do most of the work and discussion so that they're invested in their brand and communication goals. As another variation on this exercise, you can ask the participants to write on moveable sticky notes instead of directly on the whiteboard so that they can more easily rearrange the brand attributes.

Step one: define the brand offering

Label the two circles in the diagram:

- Brand values
- Audience needs

Ask your stakeholders to describe everything their brand offers or would like to offer on an *emotional* level. In other words, if it's a company that sells windows or locks or data backup systems, don't focus on the products; instead, stakeholders might mention things like "security," "confidence," and "trust." Ask the participants to start listing those qualities that the organization offers or would like to offer in the "Brand values" circle.

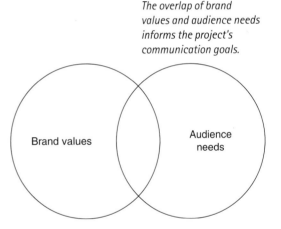

The overlap of brand values and audience needs informs the project's communication goals.

If you've got the brand attributes cards handy, they can be a useful starting point to help guide the activity if stakeholders are more reserved. Depending on the organization and industry, expect participants to list a variety of qualities and attributes:

- experience
- expertise
- always being on time
- fun
- tradition
- heritage
- innovation
- service

- creative ideas
- empowerment
- variety
- consistency

After they've filled the circle or after about 10 minutes, dig in with a few questions. As with the cardsorting exercise, you may find some obvious conflicts to discuss:

- "You say you offer both 'consistency' and 'variety.' How is that possible? Did different people add those terms?"
- "How do you offer both 'tradition' and 'innovation,' or are you trying to move away from one and replace it with the other?"
- "You listed both 'coolness' and 'trendiness.' Are they the same, or what did you mean by those terms?"

Step two: define the audience needs

Now ask your stakeholders to stop focusing on their company and offering, and instead focus on their target audience. You may be able to inform this with some baseline user research if it's available. Using the "Audience needs" circle, ask them to start listing all the qualities that their target audience wants—not just from them, but in general.

Consider the target audience for MOO. One segment comprises freelance artists, designers, and other "creative" types. What might they want?

- Consistent branding
- Visibility to new patrons and customers
- More time to focus on work instead of accounting, invoicing, and bookkeeping
- More time to focus on doing work rather than pitching it
- Immediate customer service, even late at night and on weekends
- High-quality, low-cost collateral
- Automated, full-service solutions that don't require human intervention
- Ideas for how to stand out
- Inspiration for innovative personal branding

After your stakeholders have built up a list, encourage them to take a step back. Obviously, some of the things their audience may want (like more time for work) aren't things they can provide through their products, services, or brand; erase those, or remove the relevant sticky notes. Ask them to take a look at what remains.

Step three: focus and prioritize

Do the audience needs that remain on the board correlate to any of the brand attributes they listed in the first circle? In this example, qualities like "consistency," "empowerment," "creativity," and "service" fit the bill. Move those qualities to the overlapping region of the circles. Finally, ask them to prioritize the qualities that fall into the overlap. What's most important to communicate—what will get them in the door with their audience? And what other attributes will bolster that promise?

As with the cardsorting exercise, encourage your stakeholders to group related terms and then tell you the story of those relationships and the story of those brand aspirations. Ask them what comes first, what will get them in the door, what's the highest priority—and then what comes next? Capture this in an outline or mind map and congratulate the team on their work. Moving forward, explain that you'll translate this into the message architecture that drives subsequent tactical decisions in the initiative.

DELIVERY

Though you may need to clean up specific language or add color commentary, the message architecture that you deliver will likely look very similar to these final notes, especially if you captured them in an outline. As the first deliverable after the kickoff, I usually find it's useful to remind the client how we created it, and that I based the document on *what they told me* about their brand and communication goals. There shouldn't be any surprises here. Then I ask them two big questions: did we hear you right? And is anything missing or in the wrong order of priority?

As you present the message architecture, remind your client of its role: this will inform all the subsequent tactical decisions in content and design. And while the specific words in it don't imply specific copy—any more than its black text on white paper will necessarily drive the design—it is important to make sure we get it right so as to help ensure everyone's on the same page moving forward.

OKAY, BUT WHO'S GOING TO PAY FOR THIS?

When you take your stakeholders through a process to create a message architecture, you can open the lines of communication, encourage new discussion on their brand, and bring greater clarity into your creative process. As your stakeholders wrestle and commit to prioritizing their communication goals, they may be saving you iteration on far-flung concepts that they'd only end up throwing out. Upfront investment in message architecture can really help and streamline the design process. But won't it elongate the timeline and require additional budget?

No. Hear that echoing from the halls of agencies large and small? No, no, no . . . that's because whether the design budget is a few thousand dollars or $50,000—or more, you lucky person, you!—if you can funnel off as little as a few hours to content strategy, you can save exponentially more in the design process. In a nutshell, spend money to save money. Here's how: rather than creating moodboards or Photoshop comps for initial rounds of conceptualizing, you can use a message architecture to drive the discussion more quickly and precisely. That's time you can also invest in honing the details as you get to a single design direction more quickly.

> Surprise! It's cheaper to iterate in Word than in Photoshop.

PULLING IT ALL TOGETHER WITH CONSISTENCY—AND COPY

Consider the impact of starting with a message architecture. A month after the kickoff, as you start building comps on top of wireframes, your stakeholders shouldn't be debating personal preferences in a color scheme or your choice of typeface. Instead, elevate their feedback and focus the discussion around your solid reasons. You'll be able to substantiate your decisions on a more objective basis. Take a look at the next page. Consider, for example, how you could translate the message architecture for a financial services brand.

As you explain to your client, you chose Sabon for the headlines in the comps because it best communicates the conservative qualities your client said were most important to communicate. It's a classic typeface, but not as commonplace as its relative, Garamond. It combines well with Frutiger, which you're considering for the subheads, as it's approachable and friendly without being folksy. They're reading real copy in that typeface, because your content strategist drafted sample copy that also manifests qualities from the message architecture: it uses clear, direct sentences that all start with a verb in active voice and exude confidence by addressing the audience in the second person. The wireframes behind each comp reflect similar thinking. The organization fits with users' expectations, a faceted navigation system invites the target audience to learn as they browse, and nomenclature is simple, common, and inviting. The message architecture bolsters

Message architecture

As your website redesign moves forward, we'll build on a foundation of key communication themes that appear here in order of priority. These themes are aspirational: they embody where the brand needs to go, not how it is currently perceived. The terms used in this message architecture don't imply actual copy to be used in the site, though they capture the key messages we'll try to communicate through content and design.

- Conservative, mature, and unflappable
  - Experienced and wise; has seen trends and economic cycles wax and wane
- Anticipatory and proactive in customer service and care; never reactionary
- Formal but not stiff
  - Comfortable with process

Partial implications to visual design	Partial implications to content strategy
<ul><li>Sabon for headlines, subheads, and pull quotes (treat text as image)</li><li>Enough white space so as to give the eye space to rest, but not so much the layout appears minimalist or sparse</li><li>Imagery of middle-age and older people working in understated but polished business casual attire (sweaters over collared shirts), both working separately and engaging with clients</li></ul>	<ul><li>Traditional style with accepted modern spelling (e.g., "email" not "e-mail" and spell out acronyms)</li><li>Formal punctuation (e.g., end punctuation in bulleted lists)</li><li>Slightly longer sentence structures</li><li>"Please" and "thank you" in instructional copy and calls to action</li><li>Content types like client testimonials</li><li>Longer-form executive bios</li></ul>

your comps and each one hangs together, cohesive and airtight in its interaction design, information architecture, copy, and look-and-feel.

If you've long hung your hat on *lorem ipsum*, now's the time for a team hug or *Kumbaya* singalong: you're not alone in the wilderness. Content strategy can make your life easier. Drum circle, everyone! Hurry!

While this is just a selection of the many tactical ways design and content strategy could manifest that abbreviated message architecture, you can quickly see how it could translate to cues in both look and feel as well as style and tone. There's an enormous benefit to the team: it's much easier to defend a unified, holistic *concept* than for any part of the team to separately defend discrete choices in color, imagery, diction, or content type.

E pluribus unum. Or, as Melissa Rach, Brain Traffic's vice president of content strategy, notes, "We are not competition; we are a complement." And when design and content exist in complement to each other, a cohesive, inseparable gestalt makes for a more compelling user experience.

CASE IN POINT: A USER EXPERIENCE WITH TRADITIONAL CONTENT TYPES

The content strategy and visual design of Harvard University's Alumni Club is a wonderful example of that complementary relationship.

The Harvard Club of Boston, the only Platinum alumni club of Massachusetts. Even the chandeliers support the message architecture!

While some parts of the design, such as the use of crimson, take a cue from Harvard's style guidelines, other elements clearly speak to shared communication goals. Imagery depicts the grand architecture and opulent hospitality, rather than members networking. Small caps and a sprinkling of italicized typography are elegant without being heavy-handed. Themes of exclusivity and luxury come through in content types throughout the site, such as an FAQ on reciprocal clubs, detailed dining menus, and a photo gallery of catered events. The copy telegraphs these qualities as well:

> "Whether it's a once-in-a-lifetime family occasion, the punctuation mark on a career milestone, the chance to listen to a brilliant scientist or scholar, or a game of squash, there's no place quite like the Harvard Club of Boston. Independent, nonprofit, and dedicated to our mission since 1908, we're the only Platinum alumni club in Massachusetts. When you're done browsing our site, come in and see why."

Notice the longer sentences and details that describe a life of wholesome leisure, from a "career milestone," not just a promotion, to "a game of squash," not basketball or boxing, which the Harvard Club also offers.

TAKING IT FURTHER: DESIGNING FOR USER-GENERATED CONTENT

It's easy to see how a single message architecture drives the design and content strategy of the Harvard Club's website. It incorporates traditional, common content types that don't challenge the design templates with irregularity or surprises.

But surprises, variety, and empty spaces where the audience expects copy— these are the challenges you embrace when you design experiences that incorporate user-generated content. Users might leave fields blank, fill them with obscenities, or fill them with obscenities they've carefully spaced out to avoid automated comment moderation. (Who devotes that kind of time and creativity to CNN.com article comments anyhow?) Some users draft detailed biographies for their profile pages, threatening character limits and patience, while others give us the silent treatment. It gets more interesting when we get to their avatars: your community might comprise suburban moms, new babies, and boats. And as it turns out, those boats are pretty active in the comments!

Upfront content strategy and the message architecture can help address both the issues with how users engage social features and how visual design and wireframes accommodate—and limit—the unknowns. Variety might be the spice of life, but it won't make your life as a designer any easier, no matter how flexible you envision your templates.

Consider all the variables that define specific content—even if we just limit it to a specific content type, such as a user profile:

- Size (headshot file size, dimensions, resolution; biography character count)
- Format (JPEG, EPS, PDF, DOC, etc.)
- Subject matter (user's headshot from the shoulders up, with a pet, with friends, life story, favorite quote, etc.)

Content strategy can anticipate—and accommodate and invite—the right types of user-generated content. Ancillary copy elements, such as instructional copy and field labels, help to set the tone of responses. Example or default copy and prefilled fields also help to set user expectations, while interaction design affordances can limit the structure of responses. While open text fields may welcome a variety of responses, structures such as top five pick lists and restricted taxonomies limit variety while still inviting participation.

What do we mean when we discuss the "right type" of content? "Right" varies by site or application, but it fits this profile: it conforms to social conventions and design expectations, breaking neither the usage guidelines or templates of the specific context.

Tufts University waded into this challenge in 2010. Building off the real-world tradition in which students pass candles up a hill to "Light the Hill" every year, an interoffice team worked with ISITE Design to create an online version for alumni. The Light the Hill website invited young alumni of the past decade to light a virtual candle and add their memory to a digital hill. Participants could reconnect with others while sharing content with the offices of advancement and alumni relations.

LighttheHill.com invited young alumni to share their Tufts memories—clean memories of an appropriate length and structure—through an anticipatory content strategy for user-generated content.

The stakeholder team initially hesitated about letting the recent grads post anything they wanted without moderation—but they also didn't want to hold their comments for review and delay the immediate gratification that could come with contributing. Content strategy helped allay some of those concerns.

Instructional copy helped to set the tone. "Reconnect and recall the events that defined your time here" began the central value proposition. "Share your memory and add your candle" was the primary call to action. This led to a field labeled "What's your favorite memory from Tufts?"

Alongside the field was copy that both provided a warning and helped establish rapport with the target audience. "Light the hill with your favorite memory from Tufts!" it began. "And if you recall a particularly chilly run, please, keep it clean." Like many prestigious institutions, Tufts University had an unsanctioned tradition of dubious distinction: the Naked Quad Run. An annual event, the Naked Quad Run didn't cloak its name in euphemism, nor did participants cloak themselves in anything, as they sprinted through a snow-covered campus on a designated night every December.[4] While the run may offer compelling memories, the stakeholder team didn't want the website to become filled with possibly offensive content. With a wink and a nod, they let users know what was acceptable and what wasn't.

Role model content also helped to set the tone. Before formally rolling out the site, the office invited participation from several trusted members of the target audience. At the official launch, their content was already populating the hill and demonstrating "appropriate" topics, level of detail, and character counts. That was key to successful implementation of the design: if comments were too brief, the experience might appear weak, but if submissions were too long, they would seem unreadable.

"By using the 'mavens' and seeding their example content, we set a bar for the tone and kind of content we were looking for," explained Courtney Mongell, associate director of communications and donor retention.[5] "We didn't know what to expect, but didn't want to restrict their creativity."

That thinking affected both the team's approach to governance and how they managed it day to day. Because they retained the right to review comments after posting, they rotated who was "on" to monitor comments each day.

---

[4] Though school administration previously had sanctioned this event, University President Lawrence Bacow issued a statement in March 2011 indicating it would no longer be permitted. See http://www.tuftsdaily.com/op-ed/nqr-reconsidered-1.2512697 and http://www.washingtonpost.com/blogs/campus-overload/post/tufts-president-ends-naked-quad-run/2011/03/14/ABGnjcV_blog.html.
[5] Mongell, C., Nuscher, D., and Snitow, S. (4 March 2011). Personal interview.

"The user agreement set a really high bar for what would even cause us to get involved," commented Dave Nuscher, the director of advancement and editorial and creative services. "We got an email every time someone submitted a post, and there was only one post that even moved the needle a little bit." The content strategy was working.

"We saw some references to drinking and getting naked, but it was never inappropriate," added Samantha Snitow, the assistant director of young alumni programming. "But it's college. People get naked and drink."

(Parents: note, that applies to *all* colleges.)

(Mom and Dad: note, that totally did not apply to *my* college.)

So what did the Light the Hill content strategy entail? It mapped out a way to accomplish several key goals:

- Engage young alumni
- Build visibility within their communities
- Encourage content contributions
- Facilitate viral sharing

The tactics that addressed these goals emerged from a streamlined message architecture:

- Inspire nostalgia
- Offer relevancy and clear application
- Appreciate, support, and value alumni contributions
- Provide opportunities and unique access to diverse leaders
- Be fun

Interaction affordances also helped to constrain content while eliciting engagement. With a broad range of interests, majors, and extracurricular activities, Tufts students tend to join a variety of "affinity groups," their term for student groups. The stakeholder team wanted to collect this data in a semantically useful way that wouldn't break the design. ISITE's solution? Before adding their memory, alumni could list their "*three* main affinity groups" in text fields that used type-ahead autocompletion to narrow options as they began typing. Variations in spelling or issues like multiple names for the same organization didn't get in the way of data collection, and the design team could plan ahead for the longest possible character count.

"We've used the content a ton," Dave noted, describing the impact of the campaign. "Just after the site launched, we started working with a consultant on annual giving. After three months, the consultant recommended that we needed to look at the nostalgia of our young alumni. Serendipitously, we had a bank of a few hundred quotes we could use from that group."

Ultimately, the content strategy included several major components:

- Develop a plan to engage the target audience with content they create
- Identify and implement techniques to get appropriate and consistent content
- Determine an approach to governance
- Monitor the content over time

Consider the value of collaboration between content strategy and design in this initiative. Not only could the design team craft an experience that anticipated specific content types in precise character counts, but they could also demonstrate that variety to the stakeholder team in realistic mockups every step of the way. Real content made buy-in that much easier: predictable inputs are the stuff of real copy, not *lorem ipsum*. The stakeholders could also set internal expectations for user-generated content and exert some control over it, while building a workflow and response plan to accommodate the "what if" scenarios.

As the stakeholders at Tufts knew, recent college grads have a unique capacity to offer colorful insight from the real world, especially if it features memories of a certain late-night run. In many ways, the Light the Hill initiative demonstrates the value of content strategy in the real world, in which proactive "what ifs" are always better than a screeching, collective "what now?!" And that's central to how content strategy adds value to design. It minimizes uncertainty and improves the experience for everyone: you, your clients, and ultimately, your end user.

CHAPTER 3

EMBRACING REALITY: INCORPORATING CONTENT STRATEGY INTO PROJECT MANAGEMENT AND INFORMATION ARCHITECTURE

INFORMING SCOPE AND GOVERNANCE AT JOHNS HOPKINS MEDICINE

"We focus on what we have, the resource *they* have for keeping it all up to date, and how much they *should* have." Aaron Watkins, the director of digital strategy at Johns Hopkins Medicine, described how his team handles the site reorganization requests of internal "clients" at the Baltimore healthcare behemoth.[1] Johns Hopkins Medicine is a $5 billion nonprofit global health enterprise, comprising The Johns Hopkins Hospital and more than 30 other hospitals and healthcare sites, and the Johns Hopkins University School of Medicine.

Aaron and his team serve the academic medical center's population of scientists, physicians, and students—and that's before even addressing their diverse external target audience. Though theirs is a story set in the world of healthcare, the Johns Hopkins Digital Strategy and Web Services team could just as easily work in technology, higher ed, or manufacturing. If you serve the conflicting needs of multiple internal product managers, professors with competing research interests, or the newly formed departments of an organization that's grown through acquisition, pull up a chair. You're among friends—if only because friends are people with whom you can commiserate over a stiff drink and an arduous rolling content audit.

In this chapter, I'm grouping together project managers and information architects for what content strategy can do for *you*. You play very different roles. But at a high level, you must confront a few very similar issues of scope:

- How long will this project take?
- What budget should we quote for the quantity of pages, states, screens, or modules in this experience?
- How many parts? (Pages, states, screens, modules, blurbs . . . how many rooms will be in this house?)

> When I write about "information architecture," I'm speaking to the part of you that cares about structure, organization, and categorization of content per Louis Rosenfeld's definition, "Information architecture involves the design of organization, labeling, navigation, and searching systems to help people find and manage information more successfully," and in this chapter I use it as synecdoche for the broader topic of user experience design.

---

[1] Watkins, A., Liebtag, A., and Ahava, A. (8 March 2011). Personal interview.

Project Management Institute advocates. The work breakdown structure, or WBS, follows the model in which you divide goals into activities, and activities into tasks, and then determine how long each task should take, a process project management expert Bob Wysocki describes as "decomposition."[5] "Decomposition is important to the overall project plan because it enables you to estimate the duration of the project, determine the required resources, and schedule the work," he writes. He goes on to state the obvious but elusive: "You have to define the work before you set out to do it."

Of course you do! So why does content still confound and defy project management? Because we don't do a good job defining it—and everyone's at fault:

- We assume that we fully understand the purpose of our content before we confront it in detail and assess how well it's delivering on that purpose.
- We attempt to measure it with inappropriate units, guessing at written page counts without knowing exactly what those pages need to accomplish—or if a video, customer testimonial, or photo gallery could accomplish the same thing, and if "pages" would more likely be blurbs, blog posts, or headlines.
- Most RFPs describe an end product, not its goals: they call for "a new website" or "an integrated CMS," not "a new website that helps our customers find information about billing, outages, and services from a power company they think is reliable, fast, and easy to engage."

If we don't know what our content needs to do, how will we know if it's successful?

If we don't know if it's successful, how will we know what we need to do to improve it?

So many variables affect those questions. But we started answering them in the last chapter. How will we know what our content needs to do? By assessing and prioritizing the communication goals, and documenting them in a message architecture. That's the yardstick we can use to measure existing content, at least at a high level. And initially, in the pre-sales or business development process, that may be all you need: *some* insight, a high-level but accurate estimation, is better than no insight. As the project progresses, as you move along the cone of uncertainty, you can clarify those estimates from "broad but accurate" to "narrow and precise." Content strategy helps by raising more specific questions and offering tools by which to extract and apply their answers, from business development through project execution.

---

[5] *Effective Project Management: Traditional, Agile, Extreme* (Wiley, 2009).

ASK TOUGHER QUESTIONS OF YOUR CONTENT

"How much," "how long," and "by whom" are all questions that reveal greater detail, and we need to get into those weeds to properly scope time and effort. It's also worthwhile to take them up a level to ask the bigger strategic question: "What will it take to accomplish our goals?" In some cases, communication drives those goals, and content is at the core of communication. For other experiences, transactions drive those goals, and *interaction* with content is of equal importance to the quality of the content itself. In both cases, your content strategist can help answer those fundamental questions by assessing the quality of the existing content, understanding attributes of current content types, and developing a plan to maintain or add to the content.

It's also worthwhile to dig deeper into communication goals shared by both your client and their target audience: What value proposition or brand attributes do they need to communicate? What transactions do their users need to complete or what information do they need to retrieve? Erin Kissane writes about the careful balance between the needs of the client and needs of the user, noting "User advocacy is simply a way of ensuring that a project achieves business goals."[6] If you care about your client, and care about their users, you *must* care about the content.

That leads to more questions: Is the content that's there appropriate to meeting these needs? Is it still current, relevant, and accurate to the message architecture? Is there enough of it, in the best format for the information and audience, or do you need to "translate" it, update it, cull it, or grow it?

Those questions are all too familiar to the Digital Strategy team at Johns Hopkins Medicine. They raise them as they shift between project management, information architecture, content strategy, user research, and usability testing, all within the normal challenges of a large, diverse, and political organization.

"We deal with a very siloed environment," Aaron said, detailing the many sites in the Johns Hopkins Medicine web presence. "Many people with research funding have gone out and built websites on their own over the past 10 years. It's a varied environment: Some groups have 2000 pages, others have 10. But most have faced challenges with keeping their websites up to date."

---

[6] *The Elements of Content Strategy (A Book Apart, 2011).*

The landing page of the Digestive Weight Loss Center, hopkinsmedicine.org/digestive_weight_loss_center/, represents content from over a dozen weight loss specialists: physicians, researchers, and other content creators all seek to attract their audience and share their knowledge.

Working with Ahava Leibtag, content strategist and principal of AHA Media Group, Aaron's team helps the many internal constituent groups migrate to the shared Johns Hopkins Medicine platform. In serving their internal clients, they must quote budgets and timelines, determine the workload, collaborate with their clients to develop the appropriate structure and taxonomy, and facilitate post-launch maintenance and governance.

"From the beginning, we say that their current copy is reference material for what we're planning to do. What they have, how much they should have—and the core tools we have for keeping their sites up to date," he listed off. That conversation allows them to introduce a content audit.

CONDUCT AN AUDIT THAT MEETS YOUR NEEDS

Content audits are core to the processes many content strategists employ to understand the current state of their raw materials. Using concrete standards, we try to wrap our arms around what's good, reusable, and worthy in "the old site" or existing marketing materials. You can do this too, to meet your goals.

- **Project managers:** audit for variety, volume, and quality to refine your sense of scope, and resourcing throughout an initiative.
- **Information architects:** audit to surface specific content types for more realistic and useful wireframes.

You can address these areas of focus through a range of approaches, including quantitative, qualitative, "core sample," and special-interest audits. These are not mutually exclusive techniques: many audits begin by tracking quantitative attributes, then move into qualitative details. Choose your approach depending on the needs of the project, and your phase in the project. You might need to determine a broad estimate for a budget proposal, and need to know approximately how many pages or content modules your team will address. An internal, high-level quantitative audit might give you enough information to provide a useful budget range, perhaps with levels of effort depending on what a subsequent qualitative audit reveals.

QUANTITATIVE, THEN QUALITATIVE

"Our initial audits are very high-level," Ahava explained. "Literally, what do we have? We'll list all the pages and URLs in a big spreadsheet, but there's no qualitative analysis at that stage." Listing the URLs, breaking down the content types on each page, looking for parity in their character counts . . . that's all quantitative. Some audits do this in great detail, checking to make sure all the subheads in a section are around the same length. In other cases, as Ahava described, they just need to get a gut check on the overall volume. By building a quantitative head count before moving on to a qualitative assessment, the team can determine the scope of work—how many pages or modules they'll have to touch—before determining the actual depth of engagement with that content. As they gather more information about the content, they reduce the unknowns and variables so as to minimize risk, uncertainty, and their estimate.

"I also advocate a scoring system," Ahava added. "I use a checklist based on the particulars the clients are looking for—last updated date of content, quality of web writing, SEO, etc.—and add that to the spreadsheet. The scoring system gives them a way to look at the site from a score so they get the major drift of how their site is performing in terms of content." This system also allows content owners to evaluate their content against concrete standards they deem most important, rather than unfounded opinion or standards they might brush off as irrelevant.

"After that, we'll determine their goals and the content that best supports it," Ahava continued. In this stage, they'll move into qualitative analysis. They'll assess whether current copy will uphold the new communication goals—or require translation in style, tone, message, or content type to better fit the new goals. Of course, all the work they discover will inform the project plan and budget estimate, so they don't go too far at this stage: they learn just enough so as to offer an accurate but not overly broad budget and scope to the prospective client.

This approach is one flavor of the process Colleen Jones, principal of Content Science, espouses.

"In general, doing the audit helps everyone involved understand the content situation," Colleen explained.[7] "It helps everyone get a good understanding of scope, at least at a pretty high level."

"I see the audit as a foundation you build on throughout the rest of the project," she continued. "Your initial inventory becomes a more robust audit that provides the foundation for other work: carry it through to rolling audits for really large projects, or flesh out the content matrix and site map to really solve what content is going to be part of this interactive experience." As Colleen described, many organizations run with the audit and continue to update it on a periodic basis as a rolling audit to ensure it always reflects the current snapshot of an evolving experience. It's difficult the first time, but after their initial investment, it makes sense to maintain this documentation.

The work that Aaron and Ahava do is a good example of tailoring an exhaustive—and exhausting—audit process for a team's specific needs. In order to provide an estimate to relaunch a department site in a manner consistent with the larger institution and its goals, they need to know the number of pages and currency of content as well as the level of friendliness and accessibility in tone. As an internal team that serves other internal customers, they have goals of serving those clients in an efficient, repeatable model that will allow them to deliver more consistent microsites on time and on budget. To that end, the team has developed an auditing process that allows them to minimize risk to the timeline and budget. These goals drive their audit process and clarify just how much they need to know before the project begins.

So if there's no one way to conduct a content audit, how do you determine the best way? The best approach is that which makes it easiest for you to meet the goals of your specific project. That's no small matter; confuse doing it quickly with doing it well, and you could make the mistake of embracing

---

[7] Jones, C. (27 June 2011). Personal interview.

content that's factually accurate but inappropriate in tone. You might classify content as easy to migrate, when its licensing is actually about to expire. You could aggregate content that seems similar, but actually varies greatly in length, as in the case of Paymode-X in Chapter 1. You could specify testimonial blurbs for every page, without realizing many of your client's testimonials are irrelevant to their new products and services.

Enough horror stories! Here's how to do it right: conduct your audit to the degree and level of granularity that delivers the right information to inform other activities in the project. What could that look like?

- A comprehensive quantitative audit may be necessary for you to specify work in adding content to a new content management system.
- A broad but shallow audit, spanning all categories, but only a few levels deep, might be more appropriate to help you determine all the attributes in a faceted navigation system.
- A narrow but detailed "core sample" of just a couple sections might be better if you're defining fields and options for a parametric search and need to extrapolate from there.

As with most content strategy activities, a good content audit asks that you do what makes sense for the project and your purpose. Does this sound obvious? It is—but it's something we easily forget amid pressure to "just get it done" or to sacrifice budget to flashier deliverables. One bit of advice: don't be short-sighted in your goals, or you'll pay the price in governance as you or your client attempts to maintain the user experience.

"If you invest time and effort doing it well upfront, you'll eliminate surprises and 'gotchas' and be in a better position to take advantage of opportunities," Colleen noted. Remember: while "doing it well" is subjective to the needs of your specific project, if you execute it well, you'll develop a concrete understanding of quantity and quality of your content, regardless of the audit process you follow.

What do those opportunities look like? "Let's say you conduct competitive analysis against your audit and see an opportunity to really own a topic in which your competitors don't have much content," Colleen hypothesized. "That's going to affect the focus of your project." In this case, the implications of the content audit can affect the direction of the project, not just the scope, timeline, taxonomy, and organization.

That's something with which the Johns Hopkins team is quite familiar through their ongoing audits and savvy to the institution's subject matter expertise. The team works to elevate the subjects in which Johns Hopkins has specialized

> "The IA can be part of the audit to look at potential relationships between and among content that are currently not reflected in it," Colleen commented. "If we're not doing the information architecture, we sometimes provide recommendations, like point out 'hey, we see something here that might demand a new category or need clarification.' Or 'there's way too much content in this particular area and we need to chunk it up better.' If the IA can't be a part of the audit from that perspective, the content strategist can certainly call those issues to the IA's attention."

expertise, a sort of blue ocean strategy[8] for content curation that helps them determine which topics merit a greater investment in extensive copywriting. Their audit process addresses these goals. Other teams take a more exhaustive approach or conduct the periodic, rolling audits Colleen mentioned to ensure they maintain an accurate view of the current state of their content if that best serves their goals.

"We can focus on the content types that Hopkins has access to—and specialty in—that no one else has," Ahava explained. As the *U.S. News & World Report* top-ranked hospital for the past two decades, The Johns Hopkins Hospital is ranked first in American hospitals for its specialties in otolaryngology, psychiatry, neurology and neurosurgery, urology, and rheumatology.[9] As an academic medical center and teaching hospital, it conducts research and publishes content in those areas as well. "We shouldn't always be writing reams and reams of content on topics you can find on WebMD. We should be weaving in Hopkins' unique information so that patients respond to the implicit call to action, like come see a doctor at Hopkins."

If the research and content of Johns Hopkins Medicine is a unique product, and their content strategy focuses on merchandising that product and creating more of it, it's natural to look at the results of this investment next. "We really want to track return on investment. Does it pay off to invest in this content?" Ahava asked.

Johns Hopkins Medicine isn't the only organization that determines investment by assessing the value of its content. REALTOR.org, the online home of the National Association of Realtors®, is a very different kind of organization, but applies a similar process. Their website supports a wide array of content on the myriad issues a Realtor must address: short sales, marketing, housing statistics, real estate investment, staging a house for sale, continuing education, and so much more.

"The main purpose of REALTOR.org is to keep members aware of and using the content we produce," explained Hilary Marsh, the site's managing director.[10] And with videos, online training, field guides, and other content types, that's a *lot* of content. "Every time we embark on a section redesign, we realize some of these things are so old. So we always start with a content audit. We involve

Opportunities like this could also spell an increase in budget. Project managers, this can be your opportunity to pull aside the account manager and upsell your client on new content types. Do they have testimonials, case studies, and articles about the new topic? If not, how will you get that content? See Chapter 8 for more on this and wedge services.

---

[8] Blue ocean strategy (*Harvard Business Press*) advances the idea that innovative organizations explore "uncontested market space" to develop expertise and leadership without threats from existing competition.
[9] http://health.usnews.com/best-hospitals/
[10] Marsh, H. (15 February 2011). Personal interview.

a content strategist and a user experience designer or IA to make sure they're using the same conventions as we have for other sections."

An excerpt of a REALTOR.org content audit created by content strategist Sara Zailskas.

At REALTOR.org, some of the "old content" may have historical value, as real estate policy and documentation often tells the story of social conventions, population spread, and gentrification. Hilary calls on the National Association of Realtors' internal team of librarians to help with this aspect of the content audit. "We're the ones that determine what to delete," she noted. "But some things do have historical value. We create a separate repository for this content and work with the librarians to create a taxonomy."

As with Johns Hopkins, the team at REALTOR.org uses a content audit process to inform reorganization and, at times, redesign. From a user experience and architecture perspective, audits reveal the true nature and value of what they have and how it can be of most use to their respective audiences. The librarians offer insight to evaluate content quality and recommend the appropriate structure in which to house and surface it. Does this seem arcane or infeasible? Even if you don't work in a team that includes librarians—and be jealous, because imagine how good they'd be for pub trivia nights—focus on the activities going on here. Core information architecture and content strategy activities are growing from tight collaboration and shared understanding. Erin Kissane addresses this beautifully.

"Is this an information architecture thing, or a part of content strategy?" asks Erin about the process by which a team determines the structural design and inclusivity of its content.[11] What's in, and what's out? "In my experience, it is

---

[11] *The Elements of Content Strategy (A Book Apart, 2011).*

very easy for brilliant information architects (or UX people who do information architecture) to underestimate the importance of editorial planning, voice and tone, and detailed guidelines for content creation. And conversely, it's very easy for highly skilled content people to underestimate how much information architecture has to do with things other than content: the finicky details of application behavior and interaction design, in particular. I'm a huge fan of collaborations between information architects who care about editorial concerns and content strategists who love structure and talking about data. But whatever your situation, it's important to know your way around structural design, if only so that you can provide useful feedback and support."

DETERMINE QUALITY, OR THE MANY WAYS TO TALK TURKEY

Whether we're talking about an enormous hospital system or a surprisingly extensive website for a professional association, the challenges are common. While the headcount of a quantitative audit can determine what's there, only a qualitative assessment can help you determine how good it is, whether you need to update it, and in what ways. In many ways, this is a conversation about planning the perfect meal.

This is no way to estimate your budget or page count. (Photo by Todd Dailey; used with permission under a Creative Commons license.)

All eyes are on you. Do you reach for a crystal ball to figure out the menu and determine how much to make? In dinner, as in project planning, crystal balls may reveal a mystical picture of the future, in part based on discussion of past experiences, but you can do better than that.

If you rattle off budget estimates and calculate project timelines for engagements around social media, user-generated content, website enhancements, or applications without considering the content they will employ, where you will get it, the quality of it, and a long-term maintenance plan, polish up that crystal ball. You're predicting the future with an element of risk and optimism.

Of course, you can base your estimates on the results of past work. You've made dinner before, just as you've delivered projects on time, under budget, and to the satisfaction of everyone involved. If projects are very similar in every way—in client, audience, message, goals, team, and constraints—you can simply reflect on the budgeted versus actual hours. And you likely improve the accuracy of your budget and schedule estimates with every project. Experience is an unrelenting teacher, and your "gut sense" improves with every project, client, and team member.

But planning only by gut instinct demands you risk a lot; the data of a content audit can minimize some of that risk. Content strategy can supplement what you already know well so you can estimate time and budget with greater certainty and precision. There are no guarantees in project management. But why not gird yourself with information to increase your chances of accuracy and success? Because not every project is the same, and not every meal is the same.

Let's say this is a Very Important Project, for the pinch-yourself perfect client. And let's say this isn't just any meal you're making. You're hosting Thanksgiving dinner!

Here's your challenge: how can you plan for the future if you don't know what you currently have—or what you need?

Imagine the perfect turkey dinner. The table is set to accommodate all the guests. Alongside the turkey there's a steaming dish of bread stuffing, with more on reserve if you need to refill it throughout the meal; that's everyone's favorite with this "audience." Mashed potatoes, sweet potatoes, cranberry salad, and a dish of asparagus crowd the wine glasses and water glasses and silverware. Oh, and don't forget the broccoli—lightly buttered, because though your family's health conscious, they all rave about the taste.

Congratulations! You're the hostess with the mostess—so how did you get to this point?

Easy: you invited content strategy to the table. Consider these questions in light of dinner *and* the content you'll employ:

- **What do you have?** Check in the back of the freezer, in the pantry, or on the PR server and in the online help content. Who *knows* what could be applicable?
- **Is it still good?** Dried oregano and boxed stuffing both last a long time. Vegetables? Not so much. Check homepage value propositions and seasonal landing page content for expiration dates as well. When in doubt, throw it out.
- **Do you even need it?** Another potato dish will only crowd the oven and, later, the other leftovers in the fridge. Don't call for content you can't maintain. And sushi is terrific, but might seem out of place—much like an FAQ for a topic that doesn't warrant it.
- **Do people even like it?** Why keep making the green bean casserole when your family—your target audience—doesn't like it? Tradition keeps weird stuff on our tables and unpopular content on our homepages, where it requires prep time and only gets in the way of more enriching stuff. User research and web analytics can reveal the same things about your content, as we'll discuss in Chapter 5.
- **Are you making enough?** Thanksgiving may bring surprises: some guests are newly vegetarian, some are just joining you for dessert, and some think a pecan pie will serve 10, while the person wielding the knife only cuts it into quarters.

Depending on the size of your project, you can apply a content audit yourself to elevate and answer the types of questions a content strategist would ask, or bring a content strategist on to your team to facilitate this work. Even if you're building something entirely new, an audit will still reveal what content the organization currently has and hopes to put into the new website or application. You know, the six-year-old brochures and outdated annual reports from which you can pull *perfectly* good web copy and images of employees. (What, is your client *Hotel California*? Can you assume no one ever leaves?)

At Thanksgiving or at work, what do you need your content to *do*? Don't try to budget by pages or modules if you don't yet know how many you'll need to express the main points, capture a user's profile, or complete key tasks or interactions.

Earlier in this chapter, we discussed how the Johns Hopkins team uses a quantitative audit to determine the work and scope of a project. With the metaphor of a turkey dinner in mind, I often conduct qualitative audits for a similar purpose, and use them to measure existing content against a baseline message architecture. Different projects present different challenges, constraints, and content challenges—so consider what *you* need to glean from the process.

- Learn the variety in content types so you can understand what skills will be necessary to maintain them both during and after your involvement
- Understand the options in existing content types so you can identify what will best support users' interactions and engagement in the new experience
- Get a snapshot of the volume of content you're working with, for later updates or migration
- Gain a sense of the quality so you understand what will be necessary to bring it in line with the new message architecture

Quality is a vague term, so what do we mean? This is when you and your content strategist can step back, look at the content with which you'll be working, and ask what do we have and *is this any good?* There are a few different ways you can analyze that, and translate the big, thematic questions from the Thanksgiving dinner metaphor into something more tactical and measurable.

Is it current, relevant, and appropriate?

"Good" is relative. It's easy to a marketing manager to say her team has produced a lot of good content for the website, but before you accept that verbatim, dig into the content. For the purposes of a content audit, I usually define "good" like this:

- **Is it current?** Images of products that are no longer available and video clips that forecast trends for social media, the hot new thing of 2009, will only undercut a brand that wants to project engagement, modernity, and responsiveness.
- **Is it relevant?** A children's clothing size chart can be useful on an apparel brand's website, but not in the website for their new bridge line that comprises fashion-forward business clothes for urban women. It will only dilute the focus and specificity of message.
- **Is it appropriate?** Staff head shots that feature classic styling and suits alongside third-person biographies may be recent site additions, but they won't do anything to promote a new message architecture that elevates a hip and creative culture.

Content needs to uphold the message architecture and its context, so with those standards in mind, I can easily evaluate all the content in a system. If content meets the standard for all three attributes, it fits our definition of good. If not, I identify the elements that require editing, translation, updating, or wholesale replacement. Project managers, think back to the work breakdown structure: those are activities with discrete tasks that allow us to calculate the time and level of effort.

Is it redundant, outdated, or trivial?

While that approach describes how content can qualify for inclusion, another approach determines how content can qualify for exclusion. The ROT analysis identifies content that is redundant, outdated, or trivial, and can be particularly useful if you're analyzing content and quality before a migration and need to eliminate unnecessary work. Colleen Jones describes how she conducts in the context of an audit to kick off the analysis process.

"'ROT analysis' is an existing term with which some people in information architecture are already familiar. I use it to understand the state and characteristics of the content you're looking at," Colleen explains. ROT analysis evaluates content quality through three heuristics:

- **Is it redundant?** Do landing pages preview the main topics within a category, or do they simply duplicate copy—and is that a sign subpages may be unnecessary?
- **Is it outdated?** Do "new" blog posts hail from six months ago? Do calendars of upcoming events speak in the future tense about last year's conferences? Does the website continue to hawk back-to-school products in November?
- **Is it trivial?** Do web analytics reveal zero external page views for those photos from the 2008 company softball game?

"For me, a ROT analysis is *just* the beginning. While it tells you what content is stale or woefully unimportant, it does *not* tell you what content is mediocre, inappropriate, inconsistent, or off brand," Colleen points out, explaining that she uses ROT analysis as a starting point.[12] Given your goals, your qualitative analysis can also take into account other factors.

In the *Web Site Migration Handbook*, David Hobbs, a content management and migration consultant, writes about how to "define rules for cutting the content since you want to eliminate Redundant, Outdated, and Trivial Information."[13] He encourages content owners to define hard-and-fast rules based on web

---

[12] http://www.uxmatters.com/mt/archives/2009/08/content-analysis-a-practical-approach.php
[13] http://migrationhandbook.com

analytics, sections, metadata, content sources, and the age or date of content. They might look like this:

- Remove or remerchandise any pages with fewer than 10 page views last week
- Remove any content last updated more than three months ago
- Review all content that refers to our upcoming release
- Archive any content that refers to platforms we no longer support

Before you write an automated script to take no prisoners—and make few friends—take heed. He offers that guidance with a word of caution. "Note that the quality of this data can be highly suspect, so carefully confirm that the data you are relying upon is reasonable." Do the analytics tell the full story, or do legal requirements mandate content even if no one ever visits those pages? Can you really trust the "last modified date" on a page or are there more reliable ways by which to judge currency?

He goes on to describe other attributes to use in measuring quality, some of which I've included here. While David asks these questions in the context of a content migration, you can also apply them when estimating scope in the audit for other work, such as creation, aggregation, and rewriting.

- **Does it offer strategic value?** Can the content support the "compelling vision" or message architecture outright, or do you need to "translate" it for tone?
- **Is it authoritative?** With the content at Johns Hopkins, Ahava can trust that much of it is in an area that the hospital has a unique area of expertise.
- **Does it expose stakeholders to legal risk?** Alternately, do you need to include specific content because it minimizes legal risk?

The Creating Valuable Content Checklist
With Johns Hopkins, Ahava applied yet another approach to qualitative assessment—again, tailoring it for the specific goals of her work there. She introduced the "Creating Valuable Content Checklist"[14] to evaluate whether the content met key benchmarks:

- **Findable:** Can the user find the content through metadata, linking, and appropriate tags and taxonomy?
- **Readable:** Can the user read the content thanks to a structure appropriate to the medium and message?

---

[14] http://www.contentmarketinginstitute.com/2011/04/valuable-content-checklist/

- **Understandable:** Can the user understand the content in its current content type, tone, context, use of audience-appropriate jargon, and reading level?
- **Actionable:** Will the user want to take action, spurred on by a call to action and contextually appropriate affordances like social sharing tools or comment boxes?
- **Shareable:** Will the user want to share the content because it is compelling, timely, and easy to share?

CREATING VALUABLE CONTENT™
A Step-By-Step Checklist

IS THE CONTENT:

Findable
Can the user find the content?

Readable
Can the user read the content?

Understandable
Can the user understand the content?

Actionable
Will the user want to take action?

Shareable
Will the user share the content?

DOES THE CONTENT INCLUDE:

- ☐ An h1 tag
- ☐ At least two h2 tags
- ☐ Metadata, including title, descriptors & keywords
- ☐ Links to other related content
- ☐ Alt tags for images

- ☐ An inverted pyramid writing style
- ☐ Chunking
- ☐ Bullets
- ☐ Numbered lists
- ☐ Following the style guide

- ☐ An appropriate content type (text, video, etc.)
- ☐ Reflection that you considered the user personas
- ☐ Context
- ☐ Respect for the audience's reading level
- ☐ Articulate an old idea in a new way

- ☐ A call to action
- ☐ A place to comment
- ☐ An invitation to share
- ☐ Links to related content
- ☐ A direct summary of what to do

- ☐ Something to provoke an emotional response
- ☐ A reason to share
- ☐ An ask to share
- ☐ An easy way to share
- ☐ Personalization (add hashtags to tweets, etc.)

Creating Valuable Content™, A Step-By Step Checklist, © 20011 *Ahava Leibtag. Used with permission.*

the details for every element on every page: specific content type, approximate character count or size, current messaging, etc., just as you would in a more comprehensive audit. Each element gets its own row in the spreadsheet.

This template for a core sample audit looks much like what you'd use in a more comprehensive audit.

Here, we can begin to analyze the Dining & Entertainment category of CrateandBarrel.com by specifying the content elements on the category landing page.

CASE IN POINT: VOLUME VERSUS VALUE

In 2011, a state humanities council decided to overhaul their online encyclopedia of history and cultural content. They have an enormous database comprising original articles, scans of old photographs, audio recordings, and midcentury press clippings—but volume didn't necessarily describe quality or usefulness.

If those were attributes of "good," they needed to develop a heuristic of good. I worked with the client and their web agency to establish a message architecture to determine aspirational communication goals. What qualities would the new website convey if it was "good"? In order of priority, they fell into a few buckets:

- Pioneering and innovative thought leader
  - Objective, unbiased, comprehensive content
  - In touch with current events
  - Savvy but technologically appropriate
- Professional, efficient, and effective
  - Strategic *and* tactical
  - Responsible, reliable, and trusted
- Accessible and empowering
  - Responsible and welcoming, diverse
  - Community building

Volume, or quality? You might have a closet full of clothes, but that doesn't mean they're the right size, still in style, or appropriate for a specific event. Threadbare flannel from 1994 won't work for a contemporary afternoon wedding, even in Seattle, and even if it's your favorite shirt. What content do you love but need to retire?

In the next phase of the project, we combined this with feedback and other research from their target audience—tourists, residents, teachers, and hobby historians—to determine the value of their content.

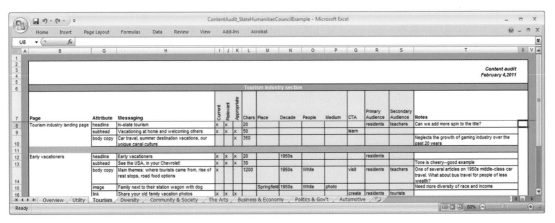

Excerpt from the content audit of an online cultural encyclopedia: there's a tab for each section in the current site, and each tab comprises rows for each element of content on each page.

Moving left to right in the excerpt, you can see how the content audit addresses quantitative factors, then qualitative factors. First, we listed everything to get the headcount, then examined the constituent parts: did every article have a title? A subhead? A related image? Are all the subheads about the same length and do they use a similar structure, or start with the same part of speech? Communication goals matter: because this nonprofit organization wanted to project their professionalism and attention to detail, content of similar types needed to be consistent.

Then we looked at the quality of that content.

- **Is it current, relevant, and appropriate?** In some cases, new and more expansive articles could subsume and replace smaller fragments. In other cases, articles might reveal too much bias from the author; the audit flags them for rewriting or "translation" in style and tone. As you can see, we evaluated this on the level of individual content elements, not just pages. Do what makes sense for your project, though in most cases, pages don't provide insight that is specific and granular enough.

We also examined the primary themes of each piece of content:

- **Place:** town or region within the state
- **Decade:** from mid-1800s through present day
- **People:** this is a dropdown list comprising women, men, LGBT, and races and ethnicities represented in the state
- **Medium:** photograph, film, poetry, painting, audio recording, etc.

These factors aren't appropriate for all audits, but as we discussed earlier, there's no one way to conduct a content audit, just a *best* way, and that will change depending on the goals of your project. Here, we wanted to understand the breadth of the current content to see if it measured up to the communication goals in the message architecture: did it successfully present the humanities council as a pioneering, empowering thought leader and comprehensive resource?

From audit to analysis to scope

The information the audit revealed fed directly into the information architecture process. At a glance, we could identify the content types that were prevalent to specific sections. Some integrated audio files, while others were heavy in photography. This allowed the team to develop a content model and wireframes that varied realistically by section along with more specific nomenclature and calls to action to introduce the content.

Project management and long-term planning also drew on the content audit. Before the audit, the client could only guess at the variety and consistency between sections; the audit's concrete data brought attention to the gaps. They could see the breadth and bias in the site because the audit captured details like the primary location in each article. By scanning the primary theme columns, they could identify where they needed to commission or curate more content and whether that would mean reaching out to an archivist, copywriter, or photographer.

In the same light, the audit helped dispel and correct some misconceptions. Stakeholders knew they had a lot of content on the state's main industry. As we realized through the audit, the bulk of that content described the early days of industry pioneers: their collaboration, groundbreakings, and contributions to the state's economy. It was fascinating stuff—but it only went through the 1980s. The political climate changed and industry competition grew in other states, but the site didn't have content to support that part of the story. Gap analysis of the audit revealed we needed to commission or aggregate content to describe how the industry was continuing to evolve and thrive through the present day.

Those misconceptions represent the gap between gut sense and glaring reality. At the right granularity, an audit can reveal an organization's politics, bias, and secret agenda.

DOCUMENT AND TRAIN FOR GOVERNANCE AND POST-LAUNCH SUCCESS

Much of the collaboration with the state humanities council follows in the steps and traditional definition of content strategy: we planned for the creation and aggregation of useful, usable, and appropriate content by establishing communication goals, assessing the content against the yardstick of those goals, and developing plans to cover the deficit. And that's where it gets interesting.

You wouldn't call a Thanksgiving dinner successful just because the right food makes it to the table, all at the same time. What earns it the badge of success is if everyone enjoyed the meal and if it brought friends and family together over good conversation.[15] In user experience design, as in the dining room, it's what happens *after* launch—and *after* you set the table—that matters most.

If you're a project manager, you know the administrative tasks of building the project plan and coordinating communication pale in value to maintaining the relationship with the client. On many accounts, the success of the relationship depends on how well you set expectations and maintain communication around them. Content strategy can help you here.

We've already discussed how the audit can inform a more realistic scope, timeline, and budget. Other tools in the content strategy arsenal can also help smooth the transition from vision through design, development, launch, and maintenance. Things like editorial style guidelines, editorial calendars, and workflow models, along with proactive teaching and ongoing mentoring, can all help ensure the end product is useful to the client as they work to make good on their communication goals.

After the launch team goes away, many organizations find the success of long-term maintenance rests in a combination of concise, specific documentation and hands-on training with ongoing mentoring.

"Historically, we've had monthly training sessions, but they were very basic," Aaron explained about Johns Hopkins' approach to departmental site maintenance. That's changing, though. "Over the past year, we've developed more online training materials: style guides, guides to the content management system, and FAQs."

This documentation doesn't replace training, but it can supplement it or allow training sessions to focus on more advanced topics.

"We've started doing more internal workshops to address more specific issues in style, use of tags, and using the CMS. We plan to expand that and eventually create a certification system: every user will have to be certified to be able to maintain their sites," he added.

Over the course of every departmental collaboration—internal "client" engagements—the Johns Hopkins web team lays the groundwork for ongoing training and post-launch maintenance. "As we're working with them, we try to

Clearly, our industry can learn a thing or two from the healthcare industry. Before you cut into my content, may I ask if you have any outstanding malpractice claims? No? Then audit away!

---

[15] Gewürztraminer helps.

develop a good relationship and stress that the web is an ever-evolving thing and we need to consistently help it grow," Aaron noted. In some organizations, the auditing process is the impetus to shift thinking from "the web is a project, finish it and move on" to the web is an asset that requires ongoing care and feeding.

HIRE AND ORGANIZE FOR GOVERNANCE

In the presentation and ebook *The Digital Deca,* web governance consultant Lisa Welchman writes about this shift.[16] She calls for 10 significant changes in how businesses embrace and engage the web. If you read between the lines in a few of those edicts, you'll see how content strategy can help you help your clients create this vision of the future. And this isn't glittering, visionary stuff; in this case, content strategy processes will offer concrete tasks you can plan, schedule, and manage to ensure previously vague goals *actually get done.*

"In a digitally transforming business environment, bold leadership is vital," Lisa writes. "Collaboration must be enabled from the top of the organization. If enabled from the bottom, power struggles will compromise business objectives."

If you skipped the section in Chapter 2 on how to use a message architecture to rally stakeholders around prioritized communication goals and a shared vision, flip back and read it post haste.

Unpack the passive voice in that. Who will do this? With what tools? Bold leadership requires vision and direction: that's your message architecture. Why are we doing this, and what are we trying to communicate? Concrete communication goals for social, mobile, and web initiatives spell out that vision in tangible, concise terms that stakeholders can evangelize and share within the broader company. If they're looking to launch a shared blog or encourage content submissions, they'll want this. The message architecture your team establishes at the beginning of the project will help maintain consistency of vision long after the project launches.

Let's look at that in the context of the US Department of Energy. The DOE spent much of 2010 and 2011 laying the groundwork for a consistent vision and new content strategy. Balancing the challenges of a staged relaunch with ongoing updates, the Office of Public Affairs worked with HUGE, Inc. to employ content strategy processes to facilitate project management, external communication, and content reorganization for the new Energy.gov and ensure the public rallied around the process. Content strategy contributed to a governance mindset.

---

[16] http://www.slideshare.net/welchmanpierpoint/the-digital-deca-10-management-truths-for-the-web-age-ebook

Comprising thousands of pages and attracting more than a quarter million page views per day,[17] Energy.gov is the primary website for the cabinet-level agency. Like the face of many large bureaucracies, the old Energy.gov focused more on the internal agency structure than the needs of its external audience. For a moment, disregard the size and visibility: there are problems here that you've probably encountered even on the websites of homegrown mom-and-pop businesses.

"We fell short in a lot of ways with our old platform," said Cammie Croft, a senior advisor and the agency's director of new media and citizen engagement.[18] "It was hard to find information; we had lots of competing information and duplicate content and a broad proliferation of redundant microsites. We competed with ourselves in search results." When an organization publishes a lot of content from multiple sources, this isn't an uncommon issue. It raises questions for the qualitative audit we discussed earlier in this section: what's good, and what's authoritative?

"We're working to streamline that user experience and put our best information forward while focusing on the information people really want," Cammie continued, speaking about the project in the spring of 2011, during an interim stage. "What you see right now is just a reskin. These cosmetic changes went a long way to show our stakeholders there's a team working on it, we know what we're doing, and to please be patient. We wanted to build support and show change was coming."

That's where HUGE's content strategy practice helped inform the approach to project management, communication, and information architecture. They had several key areas of focus:

> This is a story of a governmental agency, but it's a story shared by many teams: nonprofits with external constituents and engaged board members, organizations steeped in thorny politics and internal jargon, and distributed companies that rely on numerous content contributors in a decentralized publishing model. Central to this story is an approach to governance that let the content strategy play out over time.

- Demonstrate incremental change to maintain support, within and outside the DOE
- Enable distributed content creators to engage with the public clearly and consistently
- Make the content more personally relevant and current

"In our initial research, we realized government content needs to be personal to be useful to the individual," explained Erin Scime, HUGE's associate director of content strategy. Cammie chimed in, "A lot of the services we provide—tax credits on energy-efficient appliances, for example—vary by location. What could be available to you in Brooklyn could be different from what's available on the west coast, so we needed to be location-specific and personal."

---

[17] http://techpresident.com/blog-entry/energygov-gets-facelift-short-term
[18] Croft, C., and Scime, E. (18 May 2011). Personal interview.

The old homepage of the US Department of Energy.

As they moved toward this level of specificity, they began to reframe content around something more engaging and suited to telling the story of what they do in a variety of industries: a blog. They chose the content type not to fulfill a design need, but to better meet their communication goals. They also launched *Energy Matters*, a live-chat series with subject matter experts, and *Profiles*, a feature that uses first-person stories and rich media to illustrate the impact of energy programs on individuals across the country. The team also established a presence for the DOE on Facebook and Twitter to change perceptions of accessibility and facilitate engagement.

These were all initial quick hits to augment the content while more substantial changes were happening throughout the site—and organization. Architecture and user experience were changing behind the scenes, but so was the team that would support the new site.

"There wasn't a focus on online engagement at the DOE until the past few years," Cammie said. "I needed to build a team to focus on digital communication and how we could best reach people with the story of the work we do and why it matters. We have new media strategists and they focus on communicating across platforms about particular energy issues and areas, like renewables, vehicles, battery technology." By focusing on communicating a topic across multiple channels, rather than on owning a specific channel, strategists gain deep subject matter expertise and ensure content supports a unified experience across those channels in much the same manner as a content owner would employ an editorial calendar. Content strategy informed the plan for hiring and long-term governance.

As Cammie built the DOE team, Erin focused on how to acclimate them to the evolving site structure.

ROLL OUT EDITORIAL STYLE GUIDELINES TO MAKE THE MESSAGE ARCHITECTURE ACTIONABLE

As Energy.gov grew, the team contributing to it needed guidelines and standards to ensure they were adding to a consistent user experience.

"Standards enable collaboration. Standards for business execution must be complete and enforceable or chaos will occur with growth," Lisa writes in *The Digital Deca*. If post-launch maintenance will include content updates, your standards will need to go far beyond design templates and web standards. This is where you'll want to incorporate a rolling audit, an editorial calendar, and the editorial style guidelines—as well as the training and/or mentoring to support their successful rollout and adoption.

Editorial style guidelines deconstruct the goals of the message architecture and the task list of an editorial calendar into clear and specific templates and examples for content creation. If the calendar answers the who, what, and where of ongoing updates, the style guidelines explain how, at a level of sophistication and direction that meets the needs of the team that will be maintaining the content. For the DOE, Erin's team developed templates and guidelines to help content creators communicate effectively across channels.

> Find more details on how to create style guidelines in Chapters 6 and 7.

"It's a very large department, so there are many offices and a lot of insider jargon," Erin explained. "The site needed to represent the organizational structure, and serve the community. We standardized the office sites and gave them a templatized system to communicate with the public—and the scientists, researchers, and policy makers who go there as well."

Cammie's internal department worked to facilitate rollout and adoption so that as departments updated within the new site, the transition was smooth for both internal support staff and external content consumers.

"Our centralized team at headquarters is like a mini consultancy inside the department that provides our program offices with guidance and online strategy advice," Cammie said. "At the end of the day, a specific office is going to be better at talking about their issues, so we need to give them the tools to communicate in the space, but we work with them to best communicate and break from the more 'industry-speak.' Backend controls allow us to elevate content and distribute it in other places as well." In this way, the headquarters team acts as project facilitators and liaisons to HUGE's project managers, while affordances in the backend architecture support the content strategy's communication goals, and the content strategy drives a governance model that allows subject matter experts to flourish and communicate in an efficient manner.

Looking beyond Cammie's "mini consultancy," Erin offered content strategy support and documentation to help educate content producers in other departments. "We produced an instructional manual of how to put your pages together—the basic architecture, where you fit into it, and the templates you can use," she described. "This was used as a user's manual for training new content producers as well as a 'content style guide' to maintain quality over time and give guidance around when to use certain templates as mediums for communication in the right places," she later commented.[19] This is especially important if you want to ensure wireframes and visual design templates remain relevant. If you launch with 100-character factoids and 500-character event descriptions start to replace them in the same space, nobody wins. Help your client to not break the Internet: plan for the future with editorial style guidelines that include templates and examples.

ADD AN EDITORIAL CALENDAR TO PREPARE FOR CONSISTENCY

Find more details on how to create an editorial calendar for social media in Chapter 7.

An editorial calendar lays out the plan for how the experience will continue to change over time: who will do what, where, and at what frequency? It often addresses the complete web experience, not just the site, as it can span thematic updates to *all* channels:

- The website
- Blog

---

[19] http://www.dopedata.com/2011/08/04/energy-gov-a-content-strategy-case-study/

The evolving Energy.gov, as of June 2011.

- Twitter feed
- Facebook page
- YouTube channel
- In-app messaging
- Ads

Why go through all this? An editorial calendar offers you and your client a tactical plan for continued consistency. Beyond that concrete plan, an editorial calendar can also generate optimism the experience will take off after you kick it out of the nest. Everyone loves a happy launch, but it's the continued success that contributes to an ongoing relationship.

USE A ROLLING AUDIT TO MONITOR AND MAINTAIN

You thought we were done with the content audit? Not just yet. The tool that you used to identify variety and inconsistency can help you continue to rein it in after launch. A rolling audit builds on the initial audit to ensure the comprehensive, current view of pages or screens and the content in them remains complete and accurate. In other words, your team and your client can continue to gain value from their initial investment in the audit by spending a fraction of the time to maintain it. In some organizations, a content manager will simply go through the audit process on a periodic basis—weekly, monthly, or quarterly—in a manual or automated method to look for changes in the CMS. The benefit this offers you and your client is in subsequent projects: they'll begin with a more realistic understanding of the current state. You'll also likely encounter more confident, self-aware stakeholders.

The DOE blended the initial audit and rolling audits into a continuous process that also helped them stage the launches of many subsites.

"Don't use the term 'audit' in the federal space!" Cammie cautioned, laughing. "It means other things, and they're not usually good! We issue a 'data call' instead." Nomenclature aside, she explained how they conducted rolling content audits to more accurately estimate the scope of the massive engagement.

"There are about 16 subsites launching in the first phase. Everyone wants to say they're an office and need a website, but in some cases they really don't. We issued a website data call to get a better handle on all our online assets, consolidate our presence, and reduce redundancy. We have 85 domains and hundreds of subdomains—and we're probably a bit better than other federal agencies!

"With the data call, we capture the size of the sites, the infrastructure, and the resources allocated to them," she explained, describing how they tailored the quantitative and qualitative audit to meet the needs of a complex and matrixed organization. What did they discover? "There were low-hanging fruit we could pull onto the new platform that we wouldn't have otherwise been aware of, and we also got a better understanding of what would be more complex. We had a hunch there was a ton of redundant content, but we don't yet have the data to say that. So it's an educational mechanism as well," she concluded, noting how they continue to learn from the process.

As Energy.gov illustrates, content strategy can help a massive organization wrap its arms around unwieldy scope and move forward gracefully, with a plan for continued success. The DOE, Johns Hopkins Medicine, and REALTOR.org all demonstrate the value of a content audit in that process: project managers, content strategists, and information architects at every organization replaced hunches and platitudes with data and specificity.

In January 2011, part way through the project, Cammie blogged about how the project's progress reflected their overall business and communication goals. "Today's roll out is another significant step forward in our effort to become a more transparent, participatory and accessible Department," she said.[20] "However, we know we have a lot more work to do." With precise understanding of the content, she managed the process and looked forward to a sustainable future.

---

[20] http://blog.energy.gov/blog/2011/01/10/new-look-energygov

CHAPTER 4

EXECUTING ON CONTENT STRATEGY THROUGH COPYWRITING, CREATION, AND CURATION

KNOW YOUR STORY TO TELL IT WELL

"Our brand is very much about telling stories," began Rob Achten, the vice president of product and creative director for Icebreaker, an apparel brand based in New Zealand.[1] "Jeremy [Moon, CEO and founder] has described it like telling a story around a campfire. It's a personal story. I see the Icebreaker brand as it works on a storytelling basis. Our business model is simply different: the relationships we have with the growers and supply chain is different, so the story is unique and the way we tell it is unique. It's coated with the personalities that tell the story. Jeremy has a big impact on the tone and language used in communications. You see the catalog and the stories, and we don't use a lot of words. We tell the story succinctly, with very purposeful words, but with humor."

"Storytelling" is a compelling and organic way to describe content creation, but it belies the process and craft by which talented copywriters write articles, product descriptions, hangtags, help content, calls to action, packaging notes, marketing emails, and so much more in a way that brings brands to life and maintains cross-channel consistency over time—all with the flexibility to let the voice evolve over time.

This could be an art, an act of genius and inspiration. But for brands that distribute the work among multiple writers, or whose voice continues even after the "original writer" leaves the company, it's more science than art. As we learned in Chapter 3 with the example from the Department of Energy, style guidelines help communicate the science with how-tos, templates, and examples. At Icebreaker, Rob describes the influence of specific personalities, but also the influence of specific brand attributes on the style. Sound familiar? If you're a copywriter, you're probably familiar with balancing the art and science. Content strategy can provide some of the science to fuel your tactical execution.

---

[1] Achten, R. (11 May 2011). Personal interview.

ALIGN PURPOSE, GOALS, AND PROCESS

At Icebreaker, fluid storytelling may be the goal, but the process of creating content is methodical and focused. "Get clear on the idea: develop your story first, product second," asserts one profile about Icebreaker.[2] As a product company, Icebreaker starts with the product and the story of its raw material: merino wool.

"People had a perception of what wool was like: like what your grandmother used to knit a thick, heavy jumper.[3] So there's an educational role we had to play to teach people how merino was different from other wool and synthetic fibers," Rob said, as he started to describe the functional goals of Icebreaker's content. "There's the emotional story of where the wool comes from, but then there's the other part of the science of how merino performs. We thought it was important to put that on the swing tags."

That thinking affects not just the message architecture and tone of the content, but the salient content types as well. Online, the team focuses on decision-support content.

"We want to provide consumers with the content and features to learn and feel good about the product," Rob explained. "We're engaging with a lot of user research and user testing as we're working out the site map and wireframes and everything. How do we determine content and features? It's about finding out what works and testing it with the objective of helping [customers] feel good about a purchase."

In the crowded outdoor apparel marketplace, technical undergarments can be a commodity; consumers don't always differentiate between other brands and materials, such as synthetics like Techwick® and Capilene®, and merino wool. Icebreaker uses strategic content and specific content types to exploit the brand's differences while communicating empowerment, sustainable engagement, trust, quality, and grounding in nature.

"There's the 'born' story of how wool is born, the relationships with the farms and the merino that live in the mountains," Rob explained. "Then there's the 'worn' story—how it's worn, the benefits of the product, etc. For 'worn' content, it's led by product. The product team will come up with new initiatives, new ranges, and we'll look at messaging around the benefit for the customer. We'll try to find an angle or positioning to make it beneficial for the customer." He

---

[2] http://www.betterbydesign.org.nz/why-design/design-led-business/icebreaker
[3] That's a "sweater" or "pullover" outside of New Zealand.

went on to describe a workflow that went from the product team to include the sales team and global communications. "We'll fine-tune it with feedback from the sales team to know what resonates. Then we hand that off to [the global communications team]: they use it as a starting point and wordsmith it to make it work. They'll ask us questions, try to tease out more information. It's an organic, collaborative process within the context of a product calendar-driven process."

Beyond the raw materials, Icebreaker's New Zealand roots and "kinship with nature" set the company apart in the technical apparel category. They capitalize on this differentiator online and off. "The first 10 pages of the catalog told the story of the animal in this amazing place. We were betting that people in America and Europe found NZ—particularly the southern Alps—this inspirational place. And for our first 10 years, the story of the sheep in this environment was sort of the lead actor," Rob explained.

EVOLVE THE STORY OVER TIME

That story needed to change when Icebreaker wanted to establish a foothold in the US. Would their message and value proposition play to an American audience in which big brands dominate a crowded marketplace? Icebreaker explored the question.

"We did a project in 2010 with IDEO to explore the messaging strategy," Rob shared. "We were opening a store in New York and wanted to figure out the best way to get people off the street and into the store to try on the product. The key to selling Icebreaker is getting it on people. So we did an intensive, six-week project with IDEO where they spent time on a merino station and then went to people's homes to ask them what was in their wardrobes." As it turned out, customers said the "born" story was important, but they needed to lead with the "worn" story. Rob continued, "People wanted to know the two or three things that would have a positive impact on their lives—what's in it for them. IDEO's advice was to communicate the 'worn' benefits first and *then* back it up with the 'born' story. They created a messaging flowchart from first point of contact through post purchase when they're telling their friends about it. It was a reprioritization of the sequence."

As Icebreaker demonstrates, brands and their stories evolve over time. Sometimes, they need to meet external pressures, like industry commoditization or confusion in new markets. If you're a content creator, what does that mean to you? If a company updates its message architecture to rebrand and change how it communicates, you'll see repercussions in its style guidelines, choice of content types, and selection of themes in an editorial calendar. They'll tell the story in a different way, downplaying themes that were previously important—that's similar to the changes in messaging that affected Icebreaker.

Icebreaker's messaging flowchart reflects a content strategy with deeper roots. When Jeremy Moon launched the company, he embraced both content and product. Harvard Business School professor Joseph Lassiter describes the founder's vision: "Of his first $200,000 in seed financing, he spends a $100,000 creating a 'brand blueprint,' an architecture for what the brand needs to look like some day to exploit this advantage in natural fiber."[4] The brand blueprint specified, at a high level, how content needed to build through different customer touchpoints.

As this story evolved to meet new market challenges, the company needed to confront new questions. How did Icebreaker need to amplify and taper parts of their story? What were the implications of that sequence in terms of content types, quantity of copy, and tone? In this chapter, we'll detail how Icebreaker and other brands translate strategy into tactical guidelines to inform structure, level of detail, diction, and more—and how you can bring that thinking into your own organization.

FROM AUDIT TO ACTION

Moving from audit to content model is the act of moving from descriptive to prescriptive, from a picture of what is to a picture of what needs to be. Make that transition with a gap analysis in which you solve for x. In a way, it's basic algebra: Icebreaker had content to communicate the origins of their product, but needed more content to communicate its benefits and their unique value proposition. They solved for x with a variety of new content types.

Along the way, they didn't sacrifice the "born" story. One of the ways Icebreaker tells this is through its Baacodes: garment-specific codes that appear on the tag stitched into every item. Baacodes span content types, tying the care tag to the website, and help to elevate the story of merino's farm origins, while making tangible the ethos: "It's about our

---

[4] http://hbswk.hbs.edu/item/5203.html

relationship to nature and to each other." This content cues several of Icebreaker's core values:

- Environmental ethics
- Animal welfare
- Sustainability

Communicating the "born" story: Icebreaker apparel tags encourage the buyer to "trace the Baacode" by entering the product's unique Baacode online to "meet the merino sheep that grew this."

The simple content of a numerical code reminds consumers of the impact of their purchasing decisions and the close ties between the shirt they just bought and the sheep that contributed to it. At Icebreaker.com, consumers can enter the Baacode from a search field right on the homepage. If they don't have a Baacode—perhaps they're interested in corporate social responsibility, but haven't yet made a purchase—they can also just click to fill the field with a demo code. It's a smart bit of interaction design and content that helps fulfill the brand's communication goals.

After tracing the code, a consumer can pinpoint which of more than 100 merino stations contributed to their specific garment. Production statistics, video from the farms, and other media share the color commentary about product origins. This content doesn't ever invade the ecommerce side of the site, but it does offer a wealth of detail for the type of consumer who wants to research his or her purchase—a consumer who typifies the Icebreaker target audience.

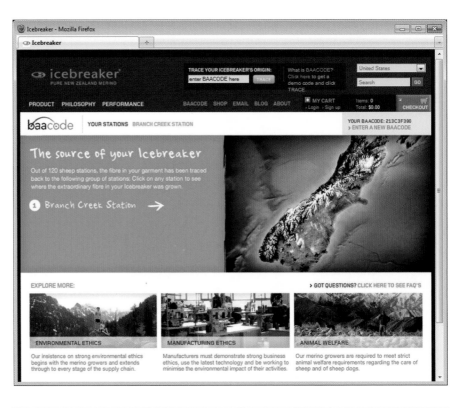

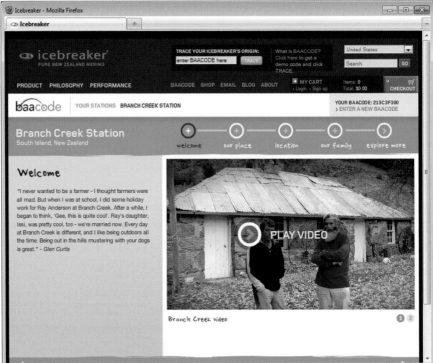

Tracing the origins: consumers can unravel their purchase from shirt to sheep—or at least farm, if not farm animal.

Icebreaker remains true to its communication goals in part by narrowing its focus. It supports many channels, online and off, but doesn't cannibalize efforts or messaging by dividing content and the resources to support it among *too* many channels. There's a lesson here, and you've probably wanted to share it more than once with an overzealous CMO. Any content you create or commission is content you have to maintain.

If you're a copywriter, you—yes, *you*—are the lucky recipient of that workload, whether it's as big as a blog or distributed as feedback in an online community. As of early 2011, Icebreaker was just beginning to incorporate user-generated content in the form of reviews on a site due to relaunch later in the year. Rob was enthusiastic about this new content, but wasn't overly aggressive about spreading out the team's creativity and resources.

"Consumers believe other consumers more than they believe brands themselves," he noted. "But more social media will come later; we know it's important, but we'll invest in it later. The website we currently have was designed seven years ago; it was set up to tell a story and be a very static catalog. It's rich in the 'born' story. The website we're designing now is more focused on commerce. The functionality and user experience will be quite different. So we're working out how we'll provide consumers with the content and features to learn and feel good about the product and make that happen." We'll get into some of those issues and discuss how social media and content strategy fit together in Chapter 7.

"How do we decide what content and features?" he asked, pausing a moment. "It's about finding out what works and testing it. Our objective is to help them feel good about a purchase."

CURATE CONTENT TO DRIVE THE USER EXPERIENCE

With a wealth of content on the web, in social media, in print collateral, and in stores, Icebreaker focuses on telling a multichannel story across a relatively small product collection each season. In large part, they can control the story. At the other end of the spectrum, some organizations juggle a broader range of content or content from multiple sources, including user-generated content. That's the case for one large television network and the niche topic domain they own.

In 2010, the television network relaunched its web presence in partnership with interactive agency HUGE. The network wanted to refocus its online purpose, communication goals, and content. They wanted to better serve engagement with the research topics in their main theme, not just the

> The CEO's blog, marketing's YouTube channel, user reviews, Twitter, the Facebook fan page, the Gowalla trip, the social responsibility microsite, the product caption contest... *this is why we drink.*

television programming that pertained to those topics, and become the foremost digital destination for information on the domain. "This was the content curation project par excellence," explained Jeffrey MacIntyre, a senior content strategist at Predicate, LLC, who contracted to HUGE for the initiative. "We needed to knit a business strategy to enterprise-level content curation for a broadcast network with untold volumes of video. It was time for them to grow up and claim what a topic-driven domain could do with engagement."[5]

"They're a television network that produces shows," added Erin Scime, HUGE's content strategist on the initiative. Though some people in their target audience visited the website to get additional details about their favorite television programs, the website's audience was changing. Their usage patterns and content expectations were evolving too, as they used the site to research topics in line with the network's theme, regardless of programming. "They had a lot of encyclopedic content, but it wasn't optimized for search," Erin pointed out. It also wasn't appropriate for broader topical research that transcended the television lineup of the largely theme-driven network. That issue fueled their main goal. "The root of the topic strategy was not only winning keywords, but becoming a destination for content that smartly juxtaposed and blended encyclopedic-style content [in their theme] with content and video clips from the broadcast show archive. Together, this package was more monetizable due to increased traffic and position in search."

TRANSLATE THE AUDIT INTO REQUIREMENTS AND TAXONOMY

As with the humanities council we discussed in Chapter 3, voluminous content, whether from an encyclopedia partner or ad platform, doesn't guarantee relevancy or quality; you might encounter a lot of out-of-date or off-brand copy. Erin and Jeffrey approached this by auditing the content, developing a new content model to integrate different content types, and working with the network to change their approach to content and production moving forward. "We helped them rethink their content offering at the level of production and programming," Jeffrey explained. "We 'atomized' everything in terms of types and formats, but we also glued it all back together in the form of coherent lifecycles for a show and topical content production and programming." They went so far as to wrangle the hands-on, tactical issues like "how to build those content types, and how to deploy and curate for them across the new site's user experience," as Jeffrey described.

Many brands face the challenge of meeting users' content expectations, even when those expectations deviate from the types of content the brand normally produces. Grace Manufacturing specializes in photoetching precision metal parts. One of their signature products is the Microplane® rasp, a favorite of woodworkers . . . and chefs. To their surprise, in the mid-1990s their rasps made the leap from shop to kitchen, and a new audience clamored for content. Now the Microplane website offers recipes that use orange zest, guidelines for storing herbs before grating, and ideas for using hard cheeses.

---

[5] MacIntyre, J., and Scime, E. (1 April 2011). Personal interview with additional discussion throughout August 2011.

Reorganizing content types, plotting ways to integrate television programming and more related research—these aren't activities that typically fall under the focus of copywriting. But as Erin and Jeffrey demonstrate, they were key steps to moving from the content audit to the new content model. Their content model, in turn, helped the network allocate resources to content creation and curation.

"We created content models that organized show content next to editorial content. That met the network's needs, especially because their holiday pages were previously their biggest search targets," Jeffrey explained. Age and the range of links and rich media on those pages had attracted search engines, but distracted from the site's new focus, value proposition, and message architecture.

"Beyond the editorial overhaul, they wanted a topic system that was prioritized to understand what keywords were winnable," Jeffrey continued. As the relationship with the encyclopedia partner was changing, the network needed to improve its access to third-party content. "They wanted us to look into the historical content universe to see what older content was out there—like old textbook publishers with evergreen content they could license." As you consider how to flesh out gaps in a content model, consider following this model. Evergreen content is timeless content that offers relevance regardless of the date or season. It's easier to curate because it doesn't demand you monitor, update, or remove it because of internal details like references to current events.

This small example offers a window into the relationship between the team's content strategists, interaction designers, and project managers, and how their processes and documentation laid the groundwork for content creation, aggregation, and curation. As the user experience grew to incorporate third-party content, Jeffrey explored and recommended new partnerships based on auditing their quality, level of detail, areas of focus, and tone. As he collaborated with the team's interaction designer, the wireframes evolved to reflect what was realistic in those new partnerships—and the structure of the content they would produce. As Jeffrey had a hand in brokering those partnerships and perspective on their content, he could inject a dose of reality to the project's timeline. The project manager also provided more value in her relationship with the client by offering counsel on those new partnerships that was savvy to their main product: new content.

As Jeffrey focused on partnerships and other aspects of the editorial strategy, Erin turned her attention to more specific areas of content strategy as we've described in earlier chapters. She began by establishing the communication

Editorial strategy activities	Content strategy activities
■ Evaluated, sourced, and licensed content vendors to understand strengths of potential third-party aggregation and curation partners	■ Created taxonomy, tags, and content model for client's editorial production team
■ Drafted high-level editorial calendar	■ Conducted content audit and gap analysis to develop production and post-launch content requirements "to chase keywords and operationally sustain the content"
■ Created style guide	
■ Developed transition plan from agency to client	

Combined work
■ Created site organization document for content manager and migration/transition team
■ Established multiple options for migrating different types of content
■ Contributed to hiring content development team under in-house content manager

Copywriting, content creation, and a long-term governance plan can all grow from this foundation of content strategy, drawing from the typical deliverables.

Prescriptive content matrix

As a bookend to (and, often, outgrowth of) the content audit, a prescriptive content matrix outlines exactly *what* content you need to create, find, and aggregate (beg, borrow, steal), and where, in appropriate detail. That detail can specify character counts, style points, keywords to include, file types, etc.

Just as there's no one way to create this kind of documentation, there's a best way, and that's the way that communicates the necessary details between the content strategist and content creators. I typically prescribe the key messages, character counts (or file type, in the case of rich media), owner, and source for content.

In Chapter 3, we discussed auditing the online encyclopedia of a state humanities council. That audit identified gaps and needs, so it looks like the spreadsheet at the top of the following page as it matures into a prescriptive content matrix.

Editorial style guidelines

If the content matrix specifies what you need to do, editorial style guidelines explain how you should do it in a way that will uphold the brand. As we'll detail in Chapter 6, style guidelines often address two main focus areas:

> Depending on the consistency we need subheads across a section, for example—I may also note the part of speech with which they need to start or other details. Depending on the culture and workflow, I may indicate owner, writer, reviewer, and manager for each piece of content as well. Do what makes sense and don't let anyone tell you otherwise.

Prescriptive content matrix
April 26,2011

Tourism industry section

Page	Owner	R1 Due	R2 Due	R3 Due	Attribute	Messaging	Keywords to include	Chars	CTA	Notes
Tourism industry landing page	Sam	6/6	6/12	6/15	headline	In-state tourism	state name, tourism	20		Add more positive spin to the title
					subhead	Take a staycation		50	learn	
		6/6	6/15		body copy	Gaming, camping, historical destinations	gaming, casino, battlefields	350		Play up growth of gaming in the state and family trips to our Revolutionary battlefields
Early vacationers	Zeke	6/6	6/12	6/15	headline	Early vacationers		20		
					subhead	See the USA, in your Chevrolet!		50		
					body copy	Main themes: where tourists came from, rise of rest stops, road food options	interstate system	1200	visit	One of several articles on 1950s middle-class car travel. What about bus travel for people of less wealth?
		7/23			image	Show family camping	camping			Need more diversity of race and income
					link	Share your old family vacation photos			create	

Overview / Utility / Tourism / Diversity / Community & Society / The Arts / Business & Economy / Politics & Gov't / Automotive

The prescriptive content matrix tells content owners what they need to create or aggregate and indicates due dates, character counts, keywords to include, and other details.

- Style, or the mechanics of construction, which includes grammar and usage
- Tone, which includes voice, tense, and messaging

When I'm putting together this type of document, I typically meet with the team members who will be implementing a content strategy to ensure I'm offering them the level of detail, range of examples, and specificity of instruction they need to succeed and manifest the voice, tone, style, preferred diction, and special structures. The style guide should communicate this, but no more or less—that's why it's key for content strategists to know their internal audiences well. Why bog down experienced writers with obvious and basic details, or confuse the already overtaxed marketing intern with abstract edicts if a simpler template would do?

If you're a copywriter new to a team with an evolving content strategy, sit down with the content strategist and share your level of expertise. Explain where you might need examples or templates. Don't be shy about helping to make this document useful and usable.

PLANNING FOR THE FUTURE

As the network's website continues to evolve, it's ready for new demands— including demands from devices it cannot even anticipate. The structured taxonomy, modular content, and a range of discrete content types are all elements of sites gearing up to meet the challenges of context and responsive design.

While this example doesn't delve into issues of presenting content on multiple devices and screens, it does offer compelling ideas and inspiration if your own work includes thinking about "responsive" content strategy, or strategy that allows you to present content so that it is relevant regardless of context, screen, and device. Designer and developer Ethan Marcotte introduced the concept of responsive web design (along with tools and examples to support it), noting that "fragmenting our content across different 'device-optimized' experiences is a losing proposition, or at least an unsustainable one."[6] While his guidance speaks primarily to visual design, it presents a philosophical corollary and call to action for content strategy as well.

How can you answer the call? Some answers lie in content management, as we'll touch on in Chapter 5, but many lie in how you create, store, and tag your content. If you take the challenges of taxonomy to their logical conclusion, you can address the contexts in which content appears far beyond just "related items." Also consider *how* it appears—images and elements it reorients or omits—when it appears in different contexts. Consider the implications for reuse, modularity, and summarization for a new 500-word article about Reykjavik cuisine that appears on the website of a travel and tourism community.

Context	Format
Website homepage	Headline as link
Website's European section landing page	Headline as link and 50-character abstract
Website's Iceland landing page	Headline, first two paragraphs, lead image, and link to continue reading
Article page on website	Headline, byline as link to more by author, complete article spread onto two pages, six images in gallery, links to four related articles, and ads for travel deals to Iceland
Mobile website landing page	Headline as link
Article in mobile browser	Headline, byline, complete article, link to gallery, and links to two related articles
Marketing email	Headline as link, small version of lead image, and 50-character abstract
Marketing tweet	Headline and link
Facebook wall post	Headline, small version of lead image, and 50-character abstract and link

These contexts assume normal desktop display; they don't even begin to follow the article to tablets and other devices—or to other sites that republish it via syndication, in the model of curation Erin and Jeffrey advocated for their client.

---

[6] *Responsive Web Design (A Book Apart, 2011).*

Through every channel, the article must maintain its internal integrity and message, even when it appears truncated or among other articles or ads. Josh Clark, a designer and developer with a special focus on mobile user experience, shared his perspective on this. "Mobile context means divorcing from format—a single format—and allowing for self-contained, discrete modularization of your content," he said.[7] Obviously, that goes far beyond just mobile phones.

Jeff Eaton and Karen McGrane describe this approach as publishing to "a reusable content store" in which your CMS supports "creating reusable content chunks that can be displayed across channels."[8] Your content can move fluidly and intelligently among channels because it is structured content, or content defined by its metadata and ready for modular reuse.

"Structure and definition allow content to be atomized," writes Rachel Lovinger.[9] "They allow the elements to be isolated and identified so that the content item can be broken down and recombined in countless variations that are free to fly to all corners of the web, across any number of devices. ..." The beauty of this approach is that it prepares content to go anywhere—including to devices and screens that don't yet even exist; as designer Stephen Hay notes, "Properly structured content is portable to future platforms."[10]

"A publisher's business is not a newspaper, a magazine, or a TV network," Rachel writes. "It's not tied to a particular format or flavor of media. The business is a brand, and it has an audience." And it's an editor or content strategist's job to communicate that brand to the target audience, to gather the right pieces to appropriately tell the story. As we've discussed, good content evolves from content strategy to tell a story and manifest its message architecture through appropriate tone and content types—whether they include original copy, curated video, or other media. Icebreaker uses content to educate its audience and improve sales, while the network uses content to position itself as a thought leader. What do you need your content to do for you—and are you taking the right steps to get there? We'll continue to address that in the next chapter as we discuss a complementary area of focus: search engine optimization.

---

[7] Clark, J. (28 July 2011). Personal interview.
[8] http://www.slideshare.net/KMcGrane/making-the-most-of-mobile-8586576
[9] The seminal report "Nimble: A Razorfish Report on Publishing in the Digital Age" (2010).
[10] http://www.slideshare.net/stephenhay/structured-content-first

CHAPTER 5

COUPLING CONTENT STRATEGY WITH SEARCH ENGINE OPTIMIZATION

TIE ONE ON FOR SEARCH ENGINES—*AND* CUSTOMERS

Gather historical trivia, how-to tips and tricks, explanatory diagrams, and blog posts about your favorite topic—or maybe your favorite brand or product. Bourbon, boating, biking, anything at all—it would be a compelling resource and probably grab a lot of your time and attention, right? That's what sites like MarthaStewart.com offer cooks and crafty homemakers. There, content attracts the target audience like bees to honey—a recipe for lavender honey, available alongside recipes that incorporate it, and ideas for honey-themed candles, costumes,[1] and cookies.

Content attracts people, who then often buy the products endorsed or created by the brand. That's easy with a brand like Martha Stewart Living Omnimedia; she started offering content long before products, as Martha published her first book nearly 15 years before launching a catalog business.[2]

But what about brands that aren't quite as ... engaging? What about brands that offer products first—and what if those products are a bit more banal than the juicy world of home and garden?

To quote *The Graduate*,[3] I just want to say one word to you. Just one word.

Are you listening?

Plastics—actually, no. Better. *Ties.*

That's the challenge Bows-n-Ties.com faces. They sell ties. Search engine optimization efforts could easily drive them to create a site in which they only say that one word, and run the risk of keyword stuffing. But high page rank doesn't necessarily lead to higher conversions—or higher customer satisfaction scores.

Instead, they've managed to create and maintain a web presence that does well by both search engines *and* their human customers, all while projecting

---

[1] What will she think of next? http://www.marthastewart.com/267222/beekeeper-costume.
[2] *Entertaining* (Clarkson Potter) was published in December 1982. Martha Stewart consolidated the publishing, broadcasting, and merchandising associated with her brand into Martha Stewart Living Omnimedia in September 1997, launching both MarthaStewart.com and the now-defunct Martha by Mail catalog that same month.
[3] Mike Nichols, Director, *The Graduate*, 1967.

a brand that's efficient, confident, and well mannered. In many respects, it is the web equivalent of a polished, middle-age salesman in a men's haberdashery who balances impeccable taste with polite, attentive customer service.

The simple but content-rich homepage of Bows-n-Ties.com, offering ties by color, as well as related accessories and usage information.

OPTIMIZE CONTENT TYPES AND TONE

The copy and content types together project this message, using a tone that's gracious and thoughtful—all while allowing for high keyword density. This is a case when the look and feel of the site is far from sophisticated, but the content itself leads the way. The homepage begins, "Thank you for visiting

Bows-n-Ties.com—your online retailer for quality men's neckties, bow ties, cuff links, and handkerchiefs. To make it easier for you to find the perfect matching tie we decided to sort our entire necktie and bow tie collection...."

A range of content types also offer opportunities to integrate keywords, link to products, and reinforce the brand in both tone and topic:

- Educational how-to pages, complete with diagrams
- A history of ties
- Care information for cleaning silk ties
- Dress code definitions and examples for black-tie weddings, interviews, and funerals
- A blog of men's fashion tips

"Your key to igniting sales," advocate Ann Handley and C.C. Chapman, "is to create online content and optimize it so that it appears on the first page of search results when your customers search for you or the products or services you sell."[4] That works for attracting prospects to your site, but only unique, engaging, and useful content and brand-appropriate content types will ensure people love the site as much as search engines do. Ann and C.C. drive this point home: "Done right, the content you create will position your company not as just a seller of stuff, but as a reliable source of information."

Bows-n-Ties.com nails this, incorporating content types that are helpful, assertive, and educational—all qualities that fit with their brand and help them grow from "a seller of stuff" into a valuable and comprehensive resource. Storage tips are helpful, the etymology of the ascot is fascinating, and recommendations for event-specific fashion are useful. They could just as easily share guidelines for craft projects involving ties—Make them into a pillow! A purse! A wreath!—but they don't, because this doesn't fit with their brand or communication goals.

The subpages further help manifest the brand through tone, topics, and level of detail. Consider the page-level copy on http://www.bows-n-ties.com/light-green-neckties.php, which clearly speaks to humans in thoughtful prose about where you might wear the product, and employs this "usage information" to incorporate keywords:

> "Ties in light green, lime, and bright apple-green are popular ties in the spring and summer. They are all colors that perfectly compliment a warm and sunny day. Below you will find all our neckties in a lighter shade of green. Besides the bright greens you will find popular wedding-greens such as fern, sage, moss, and tea-green."

---

[4] *Content Rules: How to Create Killer Blogs, Podcasts, Videos, Ebooks, and Webinars* (Wiley, 2011).

From the page-level copy on http://www.bows-n-ties.com/bowties.php, customers can learn about the appropriate tie for black-tie events, white-tie events, and more casual settings. What are the current color trends? What's the difference between self-tied and pre-tied? It's fascinating and educational, stopping just short of greeting visitors with a hearty "welcome back, my good man," a slap on the back, and a glass of sherry.

This is the perfect context for a variety of interpage links. Unlike more common "related links" or an aside of "article that may also interest you," these links are different. They're always *relevant* and applicable to the main body copy on the page. They also employ a brand-appropriate tone that goes far beyond the typical "click here." Instead, one paragraph ends "Should you still want to tie your own then our instructions on How to Tie a Bow Tie might be of help." Marvelous! No matter your sartorial tendencies, it's tough to resist clicking. Who *knows* when this information could come in handy?

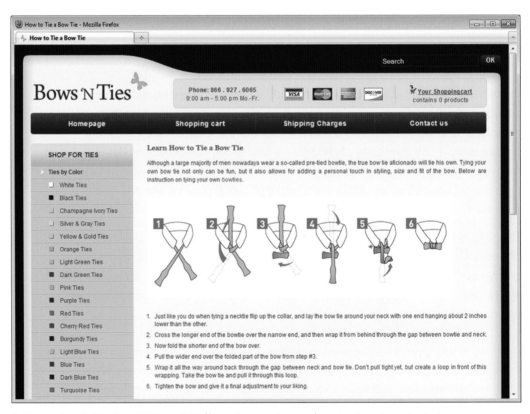

Let's learn how to tie a bow tie! (From http://www.bows-n-ties.com/how-to-tie-a-bow-tie.php.)

Like similar pages on how to tie a necktie and how to tie an ascot, the page combines several content types:

- Introductory copy about the benefits or history of the accessory
- A diagram, complete with keyword-rich alt text
- Enumerated instructional content
- Concluding copy with keywords and links to relevant products and related how-to content

Not counting metacontent or alt text, the page contains just over 500 words—56 of them include the string "tie." Though this runs the risk of keyword stuffing, the page performs well, showing up on the first page of Google results for "learn how to tie a bow tie." Not bad for a page that feels like it was written more for me than for my search engine, which hasn't been looking quite so dapper lately. Google, take note: every girl's crazy 'bout a sharp-dressed search engine.

SEO AND CONTENT STRATEGY COLLABORATION SPELLS SUCCESS

What makes the Bows-n-Ties.com content so good for both search engines and the people they serve? The harmony between SEO and content strategy enables a user experience that in which the gestalt surpasses the impact of either practice. That collaborative relationship is evolving, to the benefit of content marketing and rich content websites.

"Many SEO consultants will be tactical: they'll look at a site map, come up with a list of keywords, and put keywords into what exists and rewrite it to what they imagine search engines will favor," said Lee Odden, CEO of TopRank Online Marketing, an online marketing agency with deep expertise in search.[5] He described this fading approach, then shifted gears. "SEO expertise is now being brought into content planning itself. For example, search phrases are being combined with keyword research and being brought into the editorial plan for the site."

"It's possible to create content and tell stories *that are optimized for people first* but still incorporate the kinds of keywords they would search," he added. Though it's not a TopRank client, Bows-n-Ties.com is doing exactly that.

"Metacontent" refers to the content that describes the page for search engines. It includes keywords, a description, and title. "Alt text" is similar to metacontent in that it describes images on the page, however it's "alternate text," or a text alternative, for images, not just a supplement. If the consumer is using a screen reader or chooses not to display images, they'll need to interact with the text instead.

---

[5] Odden, L. (23 June 2011). Personal interview.

SHOP FOR TIES

Ties by Color

- White Ties
- Black Ties
- Champagne Ivory Ties
- Silver & Gray Ties
- Yellow & Gold Ties
- Orange Ties
- Light Green Ties
- Dark Green Ties
- Pink Ties
- Purple Ties
- Red Ties
- Cherry Red Ties
- Burgundy Ties
- Light Blue Ties
- Blue Ties
- Dark Blue Ties
- Turquoise Ties
- Brown Ties
- Multi-colored Ties

Special Sizes

- Extra Long Ties
- Kids Ties
- Slim Ties

Bow Ties & Accessoires

- Bowties
- Handkerchiefs
- Cuff Links
- Silk Scarves & Ascots
- Women's scarves

INFORMATION

- How to Tie a Tie
- Necktie Trivia & care Tips
- Men's Dress Codes
- Mens Fashion Tips

Primary and expanded secondary navigation at Bows-n-Ties.com. The "Ties by Color" menu is always expanded; I've expanded the "Special Sizes" and "Bow Ties & Accessories" menus here as well. Light Blue Ties? Blue Ties? Bow Ties? Bowties? Anyone?

Let's start by looking at the nitty-gritty of category nomenclature. Nomenclature in the primary navigation serves both prospective customers and search engines, as the "Ties by Color" menu is expanded to show nearly 20 categories, each of which includes the word "ties."

But users come first: this list is human-friendly, as they can easily scan down the list and see the first word in each item is the specific color. TopRank's experiences mirror this: "We'll tap into search data not just for optimizing a webpage or press release, but also in naming categories," Lee shared. "But it's consumer first. If it's doesn't resonate with the consumer, it won't get shared and it won't create conversions."

Ginny Redish advocates for this in detail in *Letting Go of the Words* (2007).

"Consider starting with a key word for fast access and accessibility," she writes, in a section on using questions as headings. She goes on to note, "If the question is short, sighted readers can see the key word that is in the middle of the question. However, people who are listening to screen-readers may not get to the key word. They often skip rapidly from heading to heading, listening only to the first few words." Just as the affordances that best serve populations with disabilities often best serve everyone,[6] links that begin with specific and different keywords serve both people using screen readers and anyone who's visually scanning down the page, rushing to find the cherry-red tie they forgot to purchase weeks ago when they first learned what color dress their date had picked for the big dance.

Link and category nomenclature is just the beginning. If you're an SEO consultant, or if you helm an internal SEO initiative, how can you bring content strategy into your work? Lee embraces the collaboration because it fuels TopRank's understanding of business impact and context. That understanding leads to better visibility, ranking, and clicks for their clients.

SHAPE SEO THROUGH THE MESSAGE ARCHITECTURE, CONTENT AUDIT, AND EDITORIAL PLAN

"People search for a variety of reasons. It's key we understand the content objectives: selling, recruiting, repositioning…key messages that reflect the needs of customer segments, what you're trying to achieve, and how

---

[6] Industrial designer Patricia Moore frequently makes this point about universal design. Consider low-carbohydrate menus for people with diabetes, thick-handled can openers for people with arthritis, and television captions for people with hearing impairments: they help and are good for *all* of us. Who doesn't want to eat more healthfully, open cans even when our hands are wet, or follow news headlines even in a noisy venue?

customers understand that. We have to understand the content plan that shows how you'll capitalize on that." Lee explained how he starts with customer personas to understand the target audience and communication goals or a message architecture.

Do you understand what your client or company is trying to communicate? While search engine analytics can reveal why the current audience is searching and visiting the website, they only tell half the story. As Lee explained, analytics don't show what you're trying to achieve or what the brand is trying to communicate. That's where you can incorporate a message architecture, as we detailed in Chapter 2. This prioritized list of communication goals can reveal if it's most important to communicate the company's narrow focus, breadth of experience, or something else entirely. A company may update its SEO efforts—and its web presence—because it's changing: it may be moving into new territory, repositioning the brand, launching a new product, or seeking a new audience. The message architecture can reveal these aspirational goals and vision of the future, while current analytics can only give you a picture of the past.

Marketo, a three-year-old business-to-business marketing company, worked with TopRank to address SEO through a process that included content strategy. "B2B marketing is a pretty big industry," Lee noted. "And they wanted to dominate their industry. They wanted to be mentioned when people talked about it."

After working with Marketo to identify communication goals, TopRank moved through a process that included a content audit and culminated in an editorial calendar. A message architecture of prioritized communication goals grounded their work; as content strategy consultant Rick Allen notes, "Objectives and goals put data in context."[7] Primed for analysis, TopRank audited the content to see if Marketo could support the new communication goals: the B2B marketing topics for which they wanted to be a go-to source of thought leadership.

"We looked at what topics they wanted to be known for and mapped [keyword] phrases to the content," Lee explained. This helped TopRank identify what content was still relevant to the new communication goals and where they needed new or additional content to support the new keywords.

"Marketo had a real commitment to content development. Jon Miller [vice president of marketing] specifically associates it with how people are now finding the site through their blog," Lee explained. Continuing through execution, the content reflects input of both SEO and content strategy

---

[7] http://www.slideshare.net/epublishmedia/making-better-decisions-with-web-analytics-4887399

perspectives, as TopRank also audited *external* content for a match with the new messaging. "We started from key messages and we prescribed and looked for a gap between those messages and the consumers' language—search terms, tweets, and blog posts. While a content strategist is going to be accountable to the key messages of the brand and company while factoring in the audience, we'll get search query data from the client's web analytics." This offers a complementary perspective, as Lee explained.

"There can be a difference between prescribed key messages and what people are actually searching for. So we'll ask: What can we do first? Can we communicate both? We may know something's an emerging concept and that [users] *will* be searching for it. So part of our editorial plan is to ensure we're first before anyone else searching for this. There's an advantage to being the first web property to be consistently ranked top for a term."

Editorial plan? Lee laughed, and explained how in addition to a message architecture, content audit, and content creation calendar, they follow a broader editorial plan to "socialize" content.

"What's increasingly effective isn't just link building," he explained. While earlier SEO techniques sought to nurture inbound links in an effort to increase popularity and ranking, it's not enough anymore. "We also want citations and mentions in conjunction with key terms. For Marketo, 'marketing automation' is the keyword. But they're battling companies that have been around 10 years in that space. It's not enough to have a plan to create whitepapers and blog posts and video; we also need to inspire conversations around that and create awareness off the website. It's about creating things that are worth sharing and worth linking to." Value and virality aren't always the same; Rick Astley can attest to that.

This editorial plan guides content quality as well, especially as Google's search ranking rewards this attention. "If someone's truly in the great content business right now, these are great times, because Google's made an effort to weed out bad content: spelling errors, bad style, lack of structure."

Content strategists often focus on the culture, workflow, and communication that sustain content production. The TopRank team incorporates this perspective as well, putting on a strategy hat to ensure multiple teams are aware of each others' efforts.

"Sometimes, we'll have recommendations from an SEO perspective, but it can be hard to put the puzzle together," Lee noted. He described a situation that happens all too frequently when SEO, content creation, marketing, and PR are

"Worth sharing" differs for every brand—and every audience. As Ann and C.C. describe so eloquently in *Content Rules*, good content "shares a resource, solves a problem, helps your customers do their jobs better, improves their lives, or makes them smarter, wittier, better looking, taller, better networked, cooler, more enlightened, and with better backhands, tighter asses, and cuter kids. In other words, it's high value to your customers, in whatever way resonates best with them."

separate silos. "Let's say SEO recommends creating a resource center with a topical hub. There are planned articles, whitepapers, and case studies for that area. But let's say there's also activity with the public relations folks—they're creating not just press releases, but video and rich media assets." In some organizations, this happens quietly, without other internal fanfare, and teams may duplicate efforts. Sound familiar?

"We'll try to tie those things together by recommending blog posts to support PR and relevant press releases from a topical perspective that we can crosslink together in a relevant way," Lee countered. "Without that, the website content might be published independently from the PR people doing press releases and blogger outreach. We can help folks make those connections and adjust timing to make a much better outcome from an SEO perspective with a content matrix mapping keywords of interest to content that exists and content that will be published elsewhere, not just on the website—even in job listings. If there's a link to additional resources, we can link the job listing to the department or product they'd support."

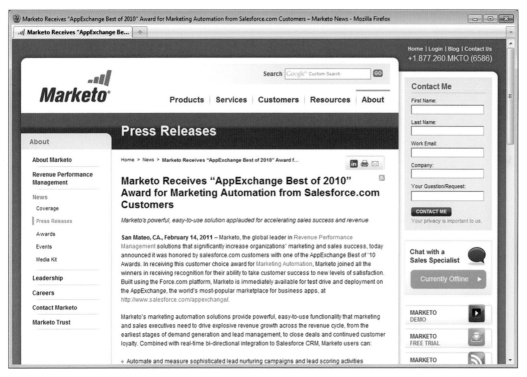

A Marketo press release reflects collaborative input from both the PR department and content strategy–savvy SEO consultants, who've tweaked the copy and added links to external sites, Marketo.com's topic pages, and top-level pages.

TopRank's approach ensures more diverse and relevant links, which are useful and rewarding to both search engines and human searchers. The effect is immediate, and long-range content planning means that it will continue. Like Bows-n-Ties.com, Marketo stands testament to the value of grounding SEO efforts in content strategy. Keywords, content types, and the overall tone uphold the brand—and pay off in visibility, conversions, and customer satisfaction.

CHAPTER 6

IMPROVING CONTENT MANAGEMENT WITH CONTENT STRATEGY

REFRAME THE CONVERSATION

"Some organizations are in publishing, so content strategy comes more naturally to them. We're an instrument of monetary policy, so it's a little different here," said R. Stephen Gracey, the manager of social media and content strategy at the Federal Reserve Bank of Cleveland.[1] In his previous role as web content manager, Stephen acted as the "chief evangelist" of content strategy for the Fed, focused on content quality control, and consulted with business areas to create and maintain timely and appropriate content.

Content management is often a technical topic, but in Stephen's capacity at the Federal Reserve Bank he also addresses cultural and human issues that are part and parcel of content management. This is the rare but right approach. Typically, discussions about content management and the content management system focus on features, cost savings, and installation. In energetic sales pitches, CMS representatives are eager to demo features, but their enthusiasm confuses the conversation and distracts from the bigger issues. Ironically, CMS discussions rarely address the content, its components, and the process by which it will be created. They don't focus on the idealized outcomes of content management, such as a better and more fluid user experience for both internal users and external customers.

As content strategist Jonathan Kahn writes, "A successful outcome [of content management] is a complex mix of achieving business objectives, implementing a content strategy, and crafting a user experience."[2] By focusing on the content strategy and these other challenges, Stephen has been able to get out ahead of some issues that normally plague content management:

- Complaints of arduous interaction with the CMS
- Forced workflow that only encourages workarounds
- Angst over having enough content to "feed the beast" of dynamic websites

---

[1] Gracey, R. S. (7 January 2011). Personal interview.
[2] http://www.alistapart.com/articles/strategic-content-management/

- Tailoring and repackaging content for different audiences
- Force-fitting content into specific modules, templates, and content types

Talking Points Memo, the award-winning and tech-savvy news organization that, just 10 years ago, was a single-author blog,[3] adeptly characterized the common pain shared by CMS users:

> "With foxhole-flashback-sincerity, they will tell you about exasperating rendering times, byzantine patch systems, the quick accumulation of idiosyncratic work-arounds and frontpages laid out by matching up 50-some-odd numbers with headlines. That's not an exaggeration. We actually lay out our frontpage by creating new blog entries—that represent headlines—linking them to the appropriate entry and then picking from a drop down menu the number of the story slot we want this headline to go in. It's like watching Roger Penrose[4] multiply with an abacus."[5]

Do these issues sound familiar? If you're starting to grimace and reflexively reach for a beer, even though it's 10 AM, you're reading this at work, and there's not a beer anywhere in the office, then I feel your pain. And I'm not a developer, nor is Stephen. We're content strategists. If you're a developer who consults in CMS selection and integration, or if you're part of an internal technical team that's eyeing a new CMS, Stephen and the other folks in this chapter can make your life easier. We'll dig in to a few stories of evolving content management to identify how content strategy can help address both the cultural and technical challenges.

First, let's talk about some of the other issues that the Fed faces. These are content strategy issues, but they can have a continual and insidious impact on content management, publishing, and organization.

ELEVATE THE VALUE OF CONTENT MANAGEMENT

"Historically, the Federal Reserve has thought of its content as publications," Stephen explained. "The switch from paper-based to electronic publications is slow, but we've made it. What we haven't caught up with is the need to

---

[3] Harvard University's Neiman Journalism Lab heralded TPM's evolution in a 2010 interview with its founder, Joshua Marshall; read it at http://www.niemanlab.org/2010/11/josh-marshall-on-talking-points-memos-growth-over-the-last-decade-moving-from-solo-blog-to-news-org.

[4] Sir Roger Penrose is an English mathematical physicist who shares the 1988 Wolf Prize for physics with Stephen Hawking. Would you force him to use a tool that could limit and delay potentially brilliant contributions to the world? Then don't do that to your internal users, either.

[5] http://labs.talkingpointsmemo.com/2011/07/the-twilight-of-the-cms.php

organize what we're writing about and how we'd schedule it because we work with a myth that economic researchers are a wild breed that can't conform to a schedule."

Identifying who does what, and at what frequency? These are basic challenges for an editorial calendar and they can affect content management as well. If your site is a mix of obsolete copy that no one knows how to update and new copy that breaks overly general templates, you know what I'm talking about.

"So, we publish when they're ready," he continued. "When we promote it well, we get lots of coverage."

"I've been making the case that their unrefined content is like crude oil, and our strategy should be to draw on that and refine it for specific audiences," Stephen concluded. His approach is a work in progress, but his central challenge is advocating for content management and proving its value in a culture that's slow to shift its publishing mindset.

Of course, who better than the Federal Reserve to question value? Stephen helps his internal content creators see the value in content strategy and content management in other work they already do. "For example, we do a lot of education. We have a group that engages with teachers to produce discussion questions and companion literature. They recognize that the spark of content strategy drives that, but it's still ad hoc to get approvals and move through the bottlenecks."

Again, this isn't a technology problem—but the CMS may get the blame if internal users can't publish to meet the needs of their specific audiences. In their culture, workflow isn't a supporting player, but rather a demanding and political challenge that drives the rate and ease at which they can produce new content. "There isn't a unified strategy; it's completely ad hoc," he added. "There's no project management facilitating the discussion or incorporating templates to drive efficiency and save money."

Driving efficiency? Saving money? These are common goals, but you won't accomplish them with just a new CMS or feature set alone. If you're jumping from your current CMS and you're ready for a new one, consider this approach. Before you start playing the field to see what other content management systems are out there, luring you with shiny new features and promises of low maintenance, out-of-the-box functionality, and a drama-free relationship, take a step back. Get to know yourself first. Or really, get to know your content.

This is a myth preserved by professionals in many fields. Creatives? Physicians? Business school professors? Don't *dare* impose an editorial calendar on them! No such expectations can tame those wild horses! I've heard this in countless industries, and always counter with this reality: busy people who value the opportunity to market their thought leadership will prioritize their writing responsibilities. However, if you cannot demonstrate the value, don't expect their investment.

Talk show–style relationship advice clearly steals a page from content strategy.

DEVELOP A CONTENT MODEL

The content model defines content types and describes the relationships between them and among their constituent attributes. "You can think of a content model as a semantic structure for content, or a database schema; it's part of the information architecture," writes Jonathan Kahn.[6] It drives how the CMS organizes, correlates, and delivers content—and can be just as high-impact as the CMS itself.

In the example of the state humanities council website we discussed in Chapter 3, the content model might include the content type "historical events." Every historical event—and as the audit revealed, there are hundreds in the database—includes the attributes of decade, city, and actor or leader. A separate but related content type could be artwork that is semantically related to the event in that it depicts it. Every artwork—all content of that type—includes attributes of title, artist, date, and medium.

We'll continue to define the website's content to understand its internal structure and semantic relationships, but the content model quickly reveals some of the challenges and functionality the CMS might need to support. Semantically rich content raises countless opportunities: should we let users link from an event to all other events that occurred in the same city? Should users be able to search on multiple variables, perhaps to find photographs from the 1930s that depict the Great Depression? Should artwork entries appear with related items from the same artist, or from the same time period?

Just as not all features are useful to your needs, not all content opportunities will uphold the humanities council's communication goals. The message architecture can focus demands on the CMS so you can evaluate options based on what's right for the brand. That's an entirely different conversation than you'd encounter in a feature demonstration.

As you get into the internal work area of the CMS, continue to collaborate with a content strategist to ensure functionality meshes with the expectations and preferences of your internal users. Go back to the content model and consider how they would add and associate content in common tasks. Does your prospective CMS natively and naturally support those processes, or would common tasks demand customization and creative workarounds? Remember, this is about making it easier for your internal audience. Your evaluation can ensure their expectations don't overextend the CMS's natural capabilities or demand too much of the budget.

That brings us back to driving efficiency. As you can see, many factors contribute to it. How can you measure efficiency if you can't yet identify the

---

[6] http://www.alistapart.com/articles/strategic-content-management/

goals of the content, who will create it, how to tag and organize it, and the usage model your internal audience expects? Draw close a colleague in content strategy. Your problem is their problem, and we need to be in this together.

CREATE A CULTURE OF SHARING, EDUCATION, AND MAINTENANCE

The Federal Reserve Bank continues to evolve a process for content management that addresses its culture, competencies, and needs. Content strategy, as the plan for the creation, aggregation, governance, and expiration of content, is the backbone of the Fed's content management, helping it stand tall and move forward in a functional, feasible way.

With entirely different expectations and processes, the same thing is happening at REI, the outdoor retailer. As of January 2011, REI.com didn't effectively employ a comprehensive commercial content management system. So many backpacks, articles about how to choose one, and videos on adjusting backpack fit, but no CMS? It's enough to make you want to curl up in your ultralight backpacking tent until springtime.

Even without a comprehensive web content management system, REI.com gets many aspects of content management right, especially in how it keeps up with demands for new and relevant content. The culture emphasizes education and drives content production. Kristina Halvorson points out[7] how the outdoor retailer employs an editorial calendar to pace content publishing while building a culture of content creation and setting expectations with employees to maintain and share their expertise. This is how the company describes its history and purpose:

> "For our more than 3.5 million active members and other customers, REI provides the knowledge and confidence to explore and discover new adventures. We do this through frequent educational clinics and expert advice at our retail stores and at REI.com from trusted REI staff who share our members' passion for outdoor recreation."[8]

In its formal "core purpose statement," the company states "We inspire, educate and outfit for a lifetime of outdoor adventure," similarly emphasizing the role of education in serving its target audience.

Customers may buy products, but REI sells the experience, products to enable it, and education to ensure their customers make smart choices and know how

---

[7] http://www.slideshare.net/khalvorson/content-strategy-ftw, originally delivered at South by Southwest 2010.
[8] http://www.rei.com/jobs/story.html

to use the equipment they buy. In addition to "expert advice" available from retail store associates, customers can find buying guides, comparison sheets, and ratings on product hangtags. And it only gets better on the website. For an ecommerce site, REI.com offers a significant amount of content for free.

A crop of REI.com/expertadvice, in which customers are invited to watch a video about how to use a GPS receiver, read an article about choosing wool clothing, print a gear checklist for backcountry snowboarding, or choose from hundreds of other resources. The content is all original to REI, created by resident experts, guides, and specialists.

Samantha Starmer, REI's manager of the ecommerce experience and multichannel space, commented on how the culture of content production and governance brings ad hoc content management into the web presence.

"We have a combination of extremely manual efforts and some home-grown stuff," she explained.[9] Though REI and REI.com offer extensive content, they're just now broaching a more formal approach to content strategy and content management. "For us, it really comes out of an explicit focus on the customer experience," which prizes education and a range of content to support products and the outdoor experience.

That's raising some new challenges as REI seeks to keep up with the variety of content their audience expects and move to a more dynamic experience.

"There are so many things we want to do: cross-pollination of content, cross-merchandising content for products," Samantha continued. Without a dynamic

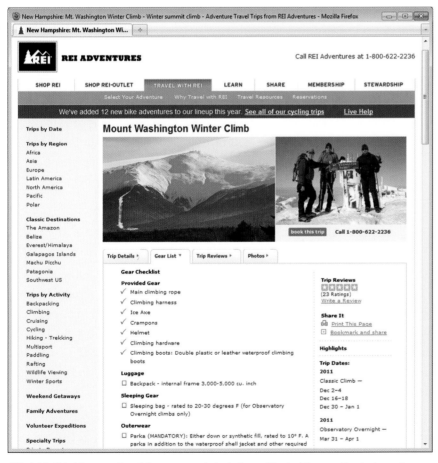

Climb Mt. Washington, site of fastest recorded wind speed in the Western Hemisphere. Better yet, do it in New Hampshire's balmy winter! REI.com/adventures recommends more than 30 pieces of gear, clothing, and accessories, but misses the opportunity to link directly to them.

---

[9]Starmer, S. (5 January 2011). Personal interview.

content management system, she's starting to see limits to the customer experience—and missed sales opportunities. "Most of what you see right now is hard-coded. If you go to our Adventures section, you'll find lists, but they don't link to product."[10]

"We have lots of really good content," she concluded. "But what's our overarching strategy? What are the content management pieces of that strategy? Much of the writing was disassociated from the UX and IA process because we only recently added those teams. We have technical writers, but the more marketing-oriented copy comes from different groups. Up until now they've had their own roadmaps, but we're working to provide connectedness and cohesion with our cross-channel communications. We have a strong brand identity, and that helps. The brick-and-mortar presence—the person in the green vest who manifests the brand—is so strong, so we're mirroring that online."

This culture of content production and brand evangelism works for REI's web presence, for now. Manual content management processes, workflow, and governance expectations help ensure the technology doesn't hold back the experience too much. But consider how your own organization is growing, possibly with content that is more multifaceted than the brand or brick-and-mortar presence itself. The Federal Reserve Bank and REI both demonstrate the strength of a publishing culture, but where does technology help take it to the next level?

CULTIVATE A CULTURE OF GOVERNANCE

REI and the Federal Reserve Bank may not have comprehensive content management systems in the traditional sense, but they do have strong cultures of content creation. That's something Oregon Health and Science University is trying to cultivate and formalize with better governance. OHSU relaunched OHSU.edu in February 2008, collaborating with ISITE Design around the information architecture, design, CMS specification, and technical implementation.

"Content matters, but only as much as you have the resources to maintain it," said Renee McKechnie in ISITE's *CMS Wisdom Report*.[11] Renee is OHSU's

---

[10] Since we spoke, this has started to evolve. After you're done reading this section, visit REI.com and see if the content's living up to its potential or could further serve their goals—and needs of the target audience.

[11] If you're in the market for a new CMS, download the report at http://research.isitedesign.com/cms-wisdom-report/ to gird yourself with the lessons of others. There's a fine line between schadenfreude and commiseration, and content management systems always seem to make you walk that line.

Manager of Web Strategies. While REI and the Federal Reserve focused extensively on acquiring new content for their respective web properties, Renee's talking more about the long term. After you get that content, who's going to maintain it—and what does "maintenance" even entail? How frequently will designated editors update it or review it to ensure it's still relevant and accurate?

You've probably seen the issues of ownership and abdication of responsibility play out in the classic example: the CEO's blog. The CEO may want a blog, or her corporate communications team may ask for one, but content is a commitment, not a trend or passing fancy. Curated content demands you maintain its relevancy, blogs demand frequent updates, and social media channels demand engagement. In Chapter 1, we discussed the example of Parallel Partner, a site in which tumbleweeds roll through the blog and "recent posts" are more than six months old. If your CMS offers a workflow module, don't assume it will *drive* and assign work. It will only facilitate the handoffs.

Renee shared her perspectives on this from OHSU.[12] "There's no point in developing great content and training CMS editors if no one is going to maintain it," she pointed out. "If people didn't have time to produce the content in the first place, chances are they're not going to return to it later. It took us two full years after the site launched to find an owner for our top-level institutional pages. The content has never been edited. We would likely have been better off with significantly fewer pages."

"We're immensely proud of the new site," she countered. "But we didn't do a good job with content ownership at first at all. We didn't have anyone to write the content—and people we did identify, some didn't know how to write or have any stake in it. They weren't a part of the project; we just asked them for content but they didn't understand the greater implications, so it never got written." This is a common issue if the CMS implementation lacks a cohesive content strategy to identify goals, cultivate owners, establish a workflow, and train on both the technical and editorial sides."

And that's where content strategy helped OHSU. The new site brought improvements in the publishing culture and workflow OHSU desperately needed. These aren't technical aspects of a CMS, but rather areas of editorial ownership a content strategist might address through training and documentation in a prescriptive content matrix or as part of the content model. Beyond the CMS, they're vital aspects of successful *content management* itself. And that's really what you're trying to achieve, right?

Where I say "editors," consider the roles specific to your organization. For too long, content hid in the passive voice: it *was published*, it *was updated*, etc. Let's put it in the active voice by assigning an owner. A content strategist will consider *who* will publish it, *who* will update it, *who* will review it (and at what frequency) to determine its relevance and currency.

In your organization, who will wear this hat? Editors? Marketing managers? Digital librarians? The marketing intern?

---

[12] McKechnie, R. (19 January 2011). Personal interview.

"After the site launched, we created a policy on site ownership," Renee explained. "All new initiatives have a technical owner and a business owner who's responsible for updating the site and providing messaging on behalf of the department or unit. We won't start a project without that."

New content management practices have also coincided with new governance initiatives that further empower the content management group.

"Also in our policy is the rule that we can take down any site if it lacks that team," Renee said. "That's a huge deal in an academic setting, but if we have a site with horribly outdated content, we can take it down. Of course, we don't want to just take sites down, so people come out of the woodwork to take ownership!"

Renee's team doesn't impose an iron-fisted, malevolent tyranny—nor would they want to; if they need to take a site down, they could encounter technical, political, and search ranking ramifications. But their policies do help ensure the website and its content best serve site visitors. Though the experience of content owners with the CMS matters, the experience of site visitors matters more. It needs to be efficient, informative, consistent, and accurate, and Renee's team makes sure of that.

Content owners, and others in the university who contribute to the site, need to feel the content culture supports them: they need access to training, accessible guidelines, time to create and maintain their content, and useful tools to do so. Without all those things, they might resent their responsibilities. Renee's team works to address this by functioning as a representative democracy. "We have a web strategies advisory committee that represents every corner of the university," she explained. "We don't just want to take sites down—we want to know these policies are right. We get together once a month and discuss the issues."

FACILITATE SUCCESS

Policy, advocacy, coalition building, and communication are all the "softer" cultural issues of content management that content strategists address under the umbrella of governance. Other elements of content strategy can affect more technical aspects of using a CMS as well.

Above all, make it easy for your internal users to produce, publish, and manage great content. Their content will drive a positive user experience for the target audience—a user experience that's current, compelling, and consistent—and that all reflects well on the value of content management (and the CMS itself) within your organization. And the positive user experience—that's a key driver, right? Twenty-six percent of content management initiatives aim to improve the customer experience first and foremost, so it's okay to say yes.[13]

So let's make it easy for your internal users. Sometimes, that just means putting the right tools at their fingertips.

EDITORIAL STYLE GUIDELINES

"I recommended they add style guidelines to each CMS template," said content strategist and editor Erin Kissane about her work on the web presence of the United States Holocaust Memorial Museum.[14] As editorial director of Happy Cog Studios, Erin participated in the redesign of the museum's website, including enterprise CMS and search functionality. She advocated the team design the CMS to prescribe specific templates, page types, and style guidelines alongside relevant modules in an effort to aid even infrequent, casual users.

Embedded guidelines aren't a typical "feature" in content management systems, commercial or custom. But if you value the user experiences of both your internal users and their prospective readers, make it easy for them to do a good job. Add cues, examples, and recommendations about the templates, style, tone, sentence structure, etc. so that they can easily manage and publish content—and create a more consistent experience for the target audience.

Editorial style guidelines detail and explain how to conform to the directives a content strategist may put forth in the content model or prescriptive content matrix, or the broad goals that appear in a message architecture, as we discussed in Chapter 3. I typically break them into two sections: style and tone. They have specific areas of focus that I tailor to the project and content:

- Style, or the mechanics of construction, includes grammar and usage
  - Acronym punctuation
  - Bulleted list style
  - Case and capitalization (Should subheads be sentence case? Title case? And what does that look like, anyhow?)
  - Numbers
  - Punctuation
  - Usage and preferred diction (Is it "website" or "web site"? Do we have "users" or "members"?)

---

[13] *Web Content Management Is Alive and Well in 2011 Thanks to Online Customer Experience* (Forrester Research 2011)
[14] Kissane, E. (4 February 2011). Personal interview.

- Tone comprises voice, tense, and messaging
  - Directional language in calls to action
  - Perspective (Should bios be written in the first person or third person—and what does that mean again?)
  - Sentence length and cohesion
  - Tense

Beyond that, I'll often include a section on "web writing 101" and additional examples for special cases—but it's entirely custom, specific to both the project and the needs of the copywriting team. That's the opportunity for the guidelines you embed in the CMS, too: if your internal users are primarily copywriters on the marketing team, they can probably handle high-level guidance. However, if the internal audience is broader and represents a range of skills, your content strategist may want to incorporate more explicit and obvious guidelines. Here's an example.

Skilled users with content expertise	General users
Event headline should start with a verb in active voice and employ sentence case.	Start the headline with a verb from the Preferred Actions list and use sentence case (i.e., capitalize only the first word and proper nouns). Examples: ■ Register now for our Volunteer-a-thon ■ Follow Mike as he blogs from the road

Erin shared more of her thoughts on editorial style with the Content Strategy New England meetup group.[15] Presenting with Mandy Brown, a cofounder and editor of *A Book Apart* and contributing editor of *A List Apart*, Erin described style guidelines as "a codification of human judgment" that enable content to "be consistent, not rigid."

"Put your tools where you can find them," Erin added. That means allowing your style guidelines to be usable and contextually relevant.

SO WHOSE PROBLEM IS IT—AND WHERE DO WE GO FROM HERE?

"CMS success hinges on your plan, your people, and your process behind your web content management initiative," according to *The CMS Myth*, a blog

---

[15] *A Pragmatic Approach to Editorial Style* (15 November 2010). http://www.meetup.com/Content-Strategy-NE/events/15312017/

that emphasizes the business strategy and cultural components to content management.[16] As we've discussed in this chapter, that couldn't be more true. But how does that play out with specific roles and responsibilities, and how are they changing in the face of new content management expectations?

"Nobody really owns how the CMS fits together," said Jeff Cram, cofounder of ISITE Design and publisher of *The CMS Myth*, commenting on the current state of content management in most organizations.[17] "It's a series of handoffs, but goes far beyond having a content strategist involved in the project—you really need folks to roll up their sleeves and figure out how it's going to fit together in execution, not just as something thrown over the wall to the developer. The developer shouldn't be the only one making the strategic decision of how content's going to fit together."

As we discussed, the culture for content management and governance is an organizational challenge; everyone owns that issue. The CMS itself can support the culture by making content management easier, and you can enable that by starting with a content model and continuing to focus on your users' needs right through implementation, training, and adoption.

You'll have other opportunities to help your internal users as you tailor the CMS. Do you need to create field labels, instructional copy, and help text? This is another time to bring in a content strategy colleague who's savvy to the message architecture and brand. "What makes sense to a developer rarely makes sense to a content contributor," Jeff cautioned.

"Very few people think about the content contributors' experience in the CMS," he continued. "Most content contributors only need to do a few things, so we need very task-driven systems—especially when you have only a few power users among many other authors." Put on your content strategy hat and consider how this needs to play out for custom development, rollout of new CMS features, and ongoing training and support. It gets expensive. "We see people design very task-driven custom content and editing experiences. They're spending a large chunk of the budget to develop task-driven custom interfaces just to edit and manage a single area."

But does it pay off?

"How do you support the occasional user?" Jeff countered. "Your best bet might be to get them out of the CMS all together and move some of your editorial processes online. The content strategist can really help by owning the

---

[16] http://www.cmsmyth.com/what-is-the-myth/
[17] Cram, J. (15 July 2011). Personal interview.

process by which you develop great experiences for internal contributors while understanding what the CMS can do to enable really specific tasks.

"The entire team needs to understand how the CMS *wants* to publish content," Jeff noted. "Every CMS has a different paradigm for content use, content storage, and content personalization. If you're living with the CMS you have, it's import for the team to go with the grain, not against it." The cultural benefits and implications to ease-of-use are enormous here. "Many organizations don't realize how to align their strategy with the technology," Jeff continued. "Yes, CMS vendors sell on flexibility, and it's true you can get any CMS to do just about anything with enough effort." But that can be expensive, time-consuming, and frustrating, especially if you invest energy in force-fitting the CMS to needs that break upgrade paths and complicate training and support. Your content strategist can help identify content needs so that you can together figure out how to manage them in ways that don't demand custom tweaks and workarounds, which can take many forms.

"A business may have the request to be able to edit any piece of content from a page-edit inline editing mode," Jeff proposed. "While many systems have this feature, there are some major limitations to it and it may not be worth the effort to get it working for all content areas. My biggest advice? Make sure someone on your team has intimate knowledge of the CMS platform and involve that person early in the strategic planning." Not just the technical implementation, but the strategic planning: What content will this need to support, how will our users want to interact with it, and what should it enable within the organization?

As user experience continues to evolve around location-based, contextually sensitive, and personalized content, content management systems need to keep pace. "We're moving into a world of content targeting and personalization," Jeff enthused. "The entire team needs to understand how personas and audience segmentation map to content delivery. It's 2011, but many sites still don't adapt to the audience. Technology is changing to allow that, but our processes need to evolve to support it too."

At Confab in May 2011, Jeff shared how content management can support contextual relevance with behavioral targeting, product merchandising, and other custom targeting rules.[18] This evolving application of content management and content provisioning demands close collaboration between a technical lead who can clarify what's possible, and a content strategy lead who can advocate for what's appropriate. (They're not the same thing.) So,

---

[18] http://www.slideshare.net/ISITEDesign/learning-to-love-your-cms

time to start making friends: the future of location-based and contextually sensitive content requires it.

But some things don't change, especially where governance is concerned. After you've made the tremendous monetary investment in a new CMS, it's silly to ignore the relatively minor investment in users that will ensure its successful rollout and adoption. The people involved in content management require training and mentoring. "How you support your web authors can make or break the success of your CMS adoption and overall website," cautions *The CMS Myth.*[19]

"There's so much effort put into planning a new website for launch, but once it launches, everyone scatters and goes on to the next big project," Jeff noted. That leaves internal users and prospective authors in the lurch. "You're starting to see full-time editorial and content strategy roles to account for this," he continued. They can employ a variety of techniques, but Jeff especially advocates adding drop-in labs in the weeks and months after initial formal training.

Drop-in labs are like office hours: they're a set time where internal users can come together in a working session with staff members who aided in the launch and have expertise in the CMS, content development, and editorial style. According to *The CMS Myth*, the labs encourage peer support while cutting the need for support in other channels, like help desk requests. By resolving frustration, they leave users feeling empowered as they use the CMS.

In many ways, drop-in labs are a microcosm of good content management itself: they're part technical, part cultural, and an opportunity for you to support your users in their success. Their success, of course, is your success. And who can help with that? Your friendly content strategist, of course.

---

[19] http://www.cmsmyth.com/2009/10/the-value-of-drop-in-labs/

CHAPTER 7

GROUNDING SOCIAL MEDIA IN CONTENT STRATEGY

MAINTAIN CONSISTENCY, CHANNEL TO CHANNEL

"We built the brand not through a pretty picture, but through content creation," began Birch Norton, a partner at BEAM Interactive and creative director of the agency's account with MINI.[1] BEAM has been working with MINI since the little car with a big heart—and an enviable turning radius[2]—first came to the US in 2001.

BEAM faced the challenge of establishing visibility and building a brand for a British BMW subsidiary that was relatively unknown in what was then the world's largest automotive market. Outside the US, it was a different story. MINI had a long history in Europe. After its launch in 1959, consumers and automotive designers alike embraced it as an icon and inspiration: its small and economical design was a sound response to the 1956 Suez oil crisis, and its groundbreaking use of front-wheel drive allowed more room for passengers and their bags in the minimal floor space.[3] Small could be smart and economical, especially in the face of uncertain access to an increasingly costly fuel source.

The 2001 MINI offered an experience its automotive ancestors only hoped for. In the 1960s, the powerful little coupe flew through the streets to win the Monte Carlo Rally several times—but as a stripped-down rally car, not a premium consumer automobile with tight handling, powerful engine, and singular design.

> Second verse, same as the first: this is a concept that could play just as well in 2001 as it could in 1959.

"A brand isn't what you tell people; it's what it does," Birch noted. "Actions speak louder than words, and for a brand, your actions are the product. But for launching a new brand like MINI, no one knew the product yet. So how could we prove this is a car not like anything else out there? It's a small car, but it's premium. You get a Porsche 911 ride for a fifth of the cost. It's got history . . . but in Europe. In the US, it has no history. You need to give people content to give them history."

If you're a social media consultant, you likely know that challenge well: just as one-to-many broadcast media demanded a message, many-to-many social

---

[1] Norton, B. (7 April 2011). Personal interview.
[2] Full disclosure: I drive a MINI and love everything about it, whether I'm zipping down the I-95 International Speedway (What? Interstate, not International? What? Not really sanctioned as a racetrack?), or deftly parallel parking along Boston Common. It handles both with spirit and agility.
[3] Though a variety of racecars featured front-wheel drive through the 1920s, the original 1959 Austin Mini is considered the first modern-day production front-wheel drive car.

media demands a framework for interaction with a multitude of messages.[4] A context and initial content, if you will, to initiate the conversation. "If you're not working to deepen relationships with [your customers] by sustaining a conversation that focuses on them, not you . . . if you don't invest in quality content that your customers will really care about . . . your competitors will," notes Kristina Halvorson.[5] For MINI, quality content comes alive in the framework of democratized opportunities for interaction, discussion, experimentation, and sharing—all to establish the company's history and newfound relevance.

START WITH A MESSAGE ARCHITECTURE

History and relevance weren't the only communication goals. MINI's social media efforts would be a stage for user-generated content, but in the context of consistent and persistent messaging from the host brand. Though BEAM developed edgy campaigns that went viral among MINI drivers, prospects, then automotive fans in general, they first needed to establish a content strategy to fuel that social media strategy.

The team rallied around communication goals that tapped into their understanding of the target audience. "People see this car in their driveway and feel more spontaneous," Birch said. That came into play as they developed a three-tiered message architecture:

> As we discussed in Chapter 2, a message architecture is a prioritized list of communication goals. These communication goals don't specify actual copy, but rather the big themes that need to come across in every channel, touchpoint, feature, and experience.

- Premium technology
- Classic design
- Cheekiness

"Cheekiness was the brand quality that drove spontaneity," Birch explained. "We never had a demographic target; we had a *mindset* target. We had bankers, creative directors, and stay-at-home moms, 25-year-olds and 55-year-olds, saying 'I don't mind standing out. I like having fun, I'm active, I value good design and what it says about me.'"

With those communication goals in mind, his team started to develop interactive content to support the mindset and drove traffic with basic email. "This was 2001, before people started really aggregating on social media sites. Our team built a database of 100 awesome swimming holes around the country, and the email didn't say 'go for a drive,' but rather 'go for a swim!'" he explained. The content kept pace with the product, as MINI added a convertible in 2005.

---

[4] Robert Scoble blogged about this way back in 2007: "When I say 'social media' or 'new media' I'm talking about Internet media that has the ability to interact with it in some way" (http://scobleizer .com/2007/02/16/what-is-social-media). This is a crude but functional and accurate description for the challenges and opportunities the channel still presents several years later.

[5] From a *ConversationAgent* interview with Valeria Maltoni, http://www.conversationagent.com/2010/12/ kristina-halvorson-content-strategy.html.

"When we launched the convertible, it was 'always open,'" he continued, referring to the tagline that acted as description—or dare. "Even if it's snowing, go ahead—keep your roof open! This was a four-wheeled motorcycle. So, we gave them a list of places around the country that are open 24 hours." Hyperbole, yes, but the audience took it to heart. This was motivation to step away from the computer, jump into the car, and explore the world . . . long before location-based services like Gowalla or Foursquare encouraged similar behavior.

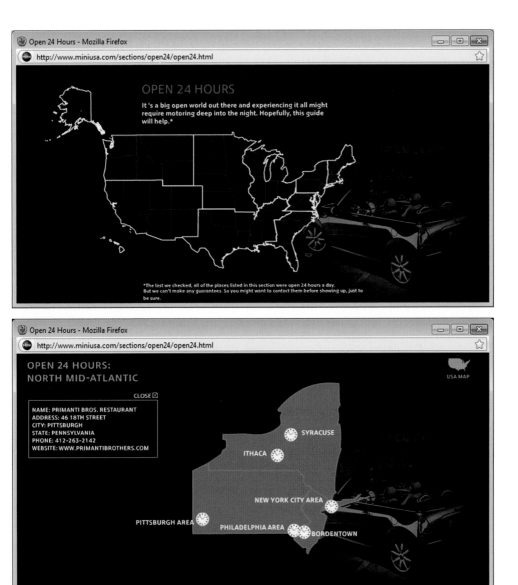

"Open 24 Hours," zoomed in to show the north mid-Atlantic region, reveals a destination in Pittsburgh's Strip District where you can drive and dine in the spirit of efficiency: the chips are in the sandwich, so don't waste your time with sides.

In both "Open 24 Hours" and the email marketing that supported MINI's campaigns, the message architecture surges through the copy. Nomenclature, calls to action, instructional content, and even legalese balance the goals of communicating the brand's premium quality with a hip, cheeky sensibility. MINI includes the mandatory opt-out language in its emails, but adds its own spin:

```
If these emails are boring you and you don't mind
missing out on all the lip-smackin' stuff we'll be
sending in the future, simply send a message to
owner-unsubscribe@insiders.miniusa.com and include
"Unsubscribe" and your favorite fruit in the
subject field.
```

> Social media and even traditional broadcast forms like email often require legal copy. That's no reason to completely break character and forget the message architecture.

Short headlines and choppy sentence structures drive an assertive, almost impatient tone, telegraphing a shared "lust for life" to the target audience. At the same time, the visual design of communications draws off the message architecture with photography that emphasizes the approachable yet cocky personality of the vehicles. Dark colors and thick, unfettered typography combine to echo the solid build quality, simple but sophisticated interior design, and unique humor of the product itself. After all, the MINI Cooper is a car that initially premiered in the US without the typical copious cup holders. When American consumers protested, MINI added a cup holder—emblazoned with a playful nod to the exuberant driver: it's marked by a symbol of a wine glass in a circle with a line through it. MINI knows the audience—and its brand voice—well. As all these decisions indicate, MINI also knows its message architecture and drives that through its content strategy.

CHOOSE CHANNELS THAT MEET YOUR COMMUNICATION GOALS—AND AUDIENCE

MINI may be slow to incorporate the more common social media channels—as of this printing, @MINI and @MINIUSA, its main US Twitter, account have fewer than 1000 tweets—but as "Open 24 Hours" and other content demonstrates, the team invests in social and user-generated content that is most appropriate to the needs of the brand and its target audience.

As you well know, organizations often have limited budgets for social media, content, and marketing, but these constraints can be empowering: limitations define the playing field and often encourage creativity. How can you rise to the challenge and make good choices with that budget? Don't just defer to the typical channels—especially if your message won't thrive there or your audience won't appreciate it there. Instead, let content strategy complement your social media strategy. As digital strategist John Eckman notes, "Strategy is just using limited resources to accomplish a goal,"[6] and in the context of social media, it's an especially important first step. In MINI's case, content strategy helps to ground the social media strategy in several ways:

- Shaping the messaging, calls to action, choice of features, and nomenclature in campaigns
- Informing the priority of new campaigns and initiatives against the message architecture
- Determining the right channels to pursue to manifest the communication goals

We'll primarily focus on that last bullet in this section. Even a big brand like MINI can't pursue every channel at once—nor should they, if they want to measure results and learn from the response to each channel. They've also focused on developing their own interactive channels, with ties to Facebook for viral attention.

Making it your own—and sharing with the world
The MINI Configurator and Custom Paint Shop both allow prospective customers to configure and customize unique features and then share their vision—and enthusiasm. "Note: What you create in the MINI Custom Paint Shop will most likely not be available at your dealership. But we know you're resourceful," is the subtle wink-and-the-gun challenge that greets visitors, who can play with Photoshop-like tools to customize their ideal MINI and share with friends—or their local custom paint and body shop.

The Configurator takes the process of envisioning, customizing, and socializing even further. "The Configurator is a key part of the online experience for MINI," Birch explained. That's *experience*, not just *sales process*, though it fuels that too, along with social marketing and manufacturing planning, which we'll detail further in a bit.

First, consider how MINI's focus on the social experience, through its investment in its own social media channels, fuels the sales pipeline, and draws so well on its content strategy. Rather than immediately jumping into the more common channels, MINI invested in building its own playing field with tools that link to those channels, allowing it to hit several important marks to ground the social media strategy in content strategy:

- The message architecture establishes clear communication goals
- A unique voice consistently underscores the brand, coming through clearly even in the cacophony of user-generated content
- A constant push of new campaigns, forums, and community engagement manifests the communication goals while keeping pace with a manufacturing-driven editorial calendar

---

[6] Eckman, J. *Don't Be a Tool: Content Management Strategy.* WordCamp Boston, 24 July 2011.

The MINI Custom Paint Shop invites prospective drivers to embrace a new canvas—and then share with friends.

MINI offers several base models, 30 body colors, roof and mirror colors, bonnet stripe options—and that's even before getting to the inside. With more than 10 million possible combinations, "more than any other car out there," according to Birch, there's a high show-and-tell opportunity. As he described, "You can share it, get feedback, and see what friends think of your configuration." With shoppers and brand enthusiasts alike playing with the tool, posting configurations to Facebook, and comparing notes with friends, the channel easily pays for itself: users engage with the product, make it their own, and hear raves from friends long before they set foot in a show room.

As users save their plans, they can route them to dealers to scope out local inventory for models that match their configurations. On a corporate level, MINI uses the configured plans to monitor trends and plan manufacturing and distribution, an approach that pays off well: as of 2011, they've been able to sell out inventory every year. The Configurator also supports further customization in the sales process, as users can access and organize the content modules into PDF spec sheets, graphical emails to friends, and downloadable desktop images—of exactly the car *they* created.

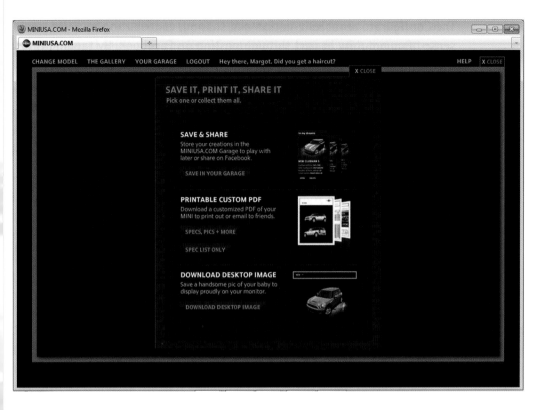

Share with friends for feedback, save to your "Garage," or print out the spec sheet to bring to the dealer—MINI makes it easy to create, socialize, and purchase your car by tailoring content types, calls to action, and functionality to the overall brand and its communication goals.

When Mick Fleetwood starts hitting the snare at the end of *The Chain*, you want to be drumming between the interior door panel and the built-in armrest.

"In Make Waiting Fun part two, we ask about your presets. How long do you want your headlights to stay on? What are your favorite radio stations? Do you want the internal dome light to stay on?" Birch listed the options, each an opportunity for the customer to express a preference. "The dealer can set all that for you." Customizable features drive the conversation, and content in branded emails and offline mailings supports that. And it's not just about the practical stuff; eager drivers receive quirky content like guidelines to take drumming the steering wheel to a whole new level, as MINI offered hints on exactly where to thump the interior to "play" along with your favorite songs.

The upshot? When drivers finally receive their new cars, they're primed to expect and engage in frequent communication with MINI, far beyond the scope of a typical transactional car shopping experience. This fosters high-touch communication and a sense of belonging, which translates into another staple of social media: the online community. As of March 2011, the MINI Owners Network included roughly 200,000 registrants, or nearly 70% of all owners. The industry average for brand-specific owners' networks is 10–15%.

PLAN FOR SUSTAINABILITY

MINI achieves quantifiable success through a combination of novelty and consistency. Content sets it apart, but it's also a challenge, and that's an area in which MINI can still improve its content strategy. "One of our pitfalls is in maintaining and sustaining content," Birch admitted. "With the 'Open 24 Hours' list, we have to ask: is that place still in business? People ping us to let us know some places have closed, but there's no budget to maintain it." Though they continue to host the microsite, he conceded it was more relevant several years ago, when the Cooper Convertible first premiered. "It had its place in time. But the more you take on for content generation, the more maintenance has to happen as well."

"Virality, PR, brand affinity, and *love* have really made the brand famous. It did what it set out to do: make a bigger splash than we imagined on the budget we had," he added, reflecting on the past 10 years. "The world's changed. Now we're focused even more on 'shareability.' First, create interesting content for people to interact with. Now, also make it incredibly portable for people to share and post around. Think syndication."

Gary Spangler, the head of corporate e-marketing at DuPont, might endorse BEAM's approach to content strategy in social media. In an interview for *Chief Content Officer*, he shared these thoughts:

"You really need to pick social channels that fit your own organization. . . . When you participate in a social media tactic like blogs, Facebook, or event Twitter, you have an obligation to keep "funding" those sites with content. . . . The networking side of social media requires a well-thought-through plan, an editorial calendar and resources to generate new content."[9]

After you know what you're going to communicate, the channels in which you'll manifest that message architecture, and the frequency and ways they relate, it's time for a few more questions. Your content strategist—or you, if you're going to put on the content strategy hat—should ask these questions of your social media strategy:

- Who will create content—posts, member profiles, tweets, Flickr galleries—to start the conversation? Who will create content to maintain the conversation or interactivity? (In MINI's case, the "conversation" could be additions to the gallery of user-generated roof graphics, which must continue to grow to appear fresh and current.)
- Who will monitor the conversation, reinvigorate, moderate, or redirect it as necessary?
- What skills should people in these roles possess?
- What rights and responsibilities do they have to engage? (Can they delete "inappropriate" images from the gallery? If so, do they need to first contact the creator? Are there standards that define what's inappropriate?)

Though MINI excelled at identifying and, often, creating channels for social engagement—a sort of blue ocean strategy to social media—features like "Open 24 Hours" exposed the difficulty of sustaining long-term initiatives without asking questions like these. In some cases, an editorial calendar might have helped them engage more comprehensively across channels, or helped with website "sunsetting" for content they could no longer support. As you'll read in the next section, this kind of long-term planning and governance can help maintain content—and brands—over time.

BUILD CONVERSATIONS WITH COMMITMENT THAT TRANSCENDS THE CAMPAIGN

AdoptUSKids approaches social media in a way that succeeds in maintaining a cross-channel experience over time, relatively free of specific campaigns. With few exceptions, their content is evidence of commitment to engagement, conversation, and their mission.

---

[9] *Chief Content Officer* (July 2011, Content Marketing Institute).

A collaborative, cooperative venture of The Children's Bureau, Administration for Children and Families, and the Department of Health and Human Services, AdoptUSKids is a nonprofit that works to raise awareness about the need for foster and adoptive families. The other half of its mission aims to help US states, territories, and tribes recruit and retain families and connect them with children. Through AdoptUSKids.org, they publish a national photo database of children in foster care who need permanent homes.

"The website was launched in 2002 to just be that photo listing of kids in foster care," Vanessa Casavant explained.[10] She's the content strategist for electronic media in the Seattle-based Electronic Media team, one of several collaborative divisions. "Now, families who are licensed to adopt can also register on the site, and they and their case workers use it like a matching system." The site also offers information on foster care and adoption for families, professionals, and the media. As of June 2011, the site included more than 30,000 child registrations and 25,000 families; 16,000 children whose pictures had previously appeared on the site now live with permanent families.[11]

This is *huge.*

When we talk about the ROI of social media, or the ROI of content strategy, we usually look for clicks, time, and dollars. Normal stuff with easy units of measure. AdoptUSKids is a grant-funded nonprofit, so they must aggressively watch those dollars; this is an example with a much smaller budget than what we just explored with MINI. But also, this is a story of content strategy–driven social media with an ROI measured in *people.* Also hard numbers—but quantitative measurements that reveal an enormous impact on children and families across the country.

CHOOSE CHANNELS APPROPRIATE FOR YOUR GOALS, RESOURCES, AND CONSTRAINTS

The story of AdoptUSKids and social media begins with a blog. The organization launched adoptuskids.blogspot.com but discontinued its use in early 2009. The format allowed them to open the lines of communication and listen to their audience, but it wasn't ideal for the topic or the frequency of engagement they needed to support. "Just because you can, doesn't mean you should," they commented in summary of the experience. Joe Pulizzi, founder of the Content Marketing Institute and Junta42, expands on this idea: "Blogs are not for

---

[10] Casavant, V. (4 August 2011). Personal interview.
[11] "Using Social Media to Engage and Support Families" (Ledesma and Casavant; AdoptUSKids).

everyone," he writes. "Blogs are pointless to use unless . . . you share. Telling important stories is only one part of it. In order to make the whole thing work, you need others to share content as well."[12]

As they shuttered the blog, they simultaneously moved to a three-headed model comprising presences on Twitter, YouTube, and Facebook. This allows them to support key parts of their mission—and key aspects of most social media engagements:

- **Lend support** through responses to frustration on Twitter
- **Build community** through open questions on the Facebook wall that encourage sharing between adoptive parents and between case workers and parents
- **Engage in outreach** and share information that addresses misconceptions about fostering and adoption processes
- **Recruit participants** through featured content

"Featured content" is a vague term here, but it plays out in significant ways for AdoptUSKids. The organization spotlights different children each week. Of the more than 700 children that have been featured since 2003, more than half have been placed in permanent families. Profile views jump over 40 times in the week a child is featured.

That is all evidence of—and to the partial credit of—a smart, content strategy–driven social media strategy. Can we give credit entirely to content strategy? No, of course not. But we wouldn't want to; after all, this is a book about how you can use content strategy in the context of what you're already doing, not just for its own virtues. In this case, content strategy drives the focus, priority, frequency, and voice of social media. AdoptUSKids monitors analytics in Facebook Insights, Klout, Google Analytics, Twitter Analyzer, and Tweet Effect to constantly review and hone their efforts. From the types and topics of posts to the time of day and geographic regions in which they were most popular, the team can see what content works best to continuously improve the experience for their target audience.

COORDINATE CROSS-CHANNEL STYLE WITH EDITORIAL GUIDELINES

As we discussed in Chapter 3, editorial style guidelines can help ensure your brand evolves consistently across channels. When AdoptUSKids features a child, its audience of prospective families and caseworkers encounters the content through multiple channels. With the caseworker's

---

[12] http://www.business2community.com/social-media/not-everyone-needs-a-blog-046683

permission, multiple tweets invite followers to the child's profile while a longer introduction spotlights similar content, along with a photo, on the AdoptUSKids.org homepage.

Tweet from @AdoptUSKids featuring Raven, a 13-year-old girl in Washington.

At the same time, if the child's caseworker allows it, AdoptUSKids posts to its Facebook wall content that mirrors the content that appeared on its homepage: the child's photo, name, age, state, all in the context of a brief description and call to action. The Facebook post also pulls additional copy from the longer listing, typically describing the child's personality and hobbies. Fans can add comments to share their enthusiasm and encouragement.

Featured photo listings offer obvious opportunities for cross-channel consistency, which succeeds due to a strong strategic foundation behind the scenes. Vanessa explained the multiple components that help ensure a seamless, consistent web presence that may span many touchpoints.

"We created style guidelines that we based off the Department of Health and Human Services online style guide," she began. "We used that as a base, and then looked at the common words we use in adoption and foster care and added those." As we discussed in Chapter 6, an editorial style guide can often include a list of preferred nomenclature (with approved spelling and spacing) to ensure consistency between writers. AdoptUSKids takes this one step further by using the custom stylebook functionality in the *AP Stylebook Online*. "We follow AP style, so we use the *AP Style Guide*," Vanessa explained. "You can build right alongside it online, and anyone in the collaboration can log in and see the most up-to-date version."

AP Associated Press

▸ Site Map   ▸ FAQ   ▸ Contact Us   ▸ Log Out

Quick Search [   ] ▸ Advanced Search

Welcome AdoptUSKids! Today is Wednesday, August 31, 2011   Font Size: ✚ ▬ ℝ

Home > Site License Entries

Search
Advanced Search
Recent Searches
Search Settings

AP Stylebook
View by Chapter
New Entries
Recent Changes
Email Alerts
View Style Categories
Online Law Guide
Corporate Profiles
Broadcast Style Entries
Online-only Entries

Org. Stylebook
Add a New Entry
Custom Stylebook
Custom AP Stylebook
Notes

Manage Users
Manage Your
Subscribers
Add a New User

Pronunciation
Pronunciation Guide
Most Recent
General
Places
People
Government
Sports

Ask the Editor
Frequently Asked
Questions
Search Archive
View Complete Archive
View My Questions
Submit a Question

My Account
Account Manager
Search Settings
Screen Settings
Update Email Address
Change Username
Change Password

Editor Entries

Site Stylebook Download File

<<Prev | 1 | 2 | 3 | **4**
Total records: 65

titles

- *Professional titles*: a person's full professional title should be capitalized without abbreviation before their name; lowercase without abbreviation and separated by a comma after their name *(HHS/AP Style)*

  ○ **Example:** AdoptUSKids Project Director Kathy Ledesma; or Kathy Ledesma, project director of AdoptUSKids
  ○ **Exceptions:** when listing names for presentations, events, etc.

- Accepted abbreviations for professional titles preceding a name include Gov., Lt. Gov., Rep., Sen. and certain military ranks *(HHS Style)*

- If a person is in an acting position, include the word acting as part of their official title and follow the capitalization rules above (HHS Style)

- *Publications, books, reports, etc*: always use italics and capitalize the principal words, including prepositions and conjunctions with more than four letters and articles of speech with four letters or less when it is the first or last word in a title *(AP Style)* (see also italics)

  ○ **Example:** Finding Common Ground: A Guide for Child Welfare Agencies Working with Communities of Faith

- Titles of chapters and articles within a larger publication are written in quotations marks without italics *(AP Style)*

- *academic degrees*: (see academic degrees)

tone of voice

Federal Plain Language Guidelines must be followed for all AdoptUSKids materials.

An excerpt from the AdoptUSKids style guide, a version of the AP Stylebook Online customized with relevant examples and notes.

Because their style points live alongside the more general style guidelines, the 50+ writers and contributors from AdoptUSKids gain a couple key benefits:

- All style and tone guidelines are in a single, authoritative source
- As the style evolves or the Electronic Media team adds new terminology, the web ensures all writers have access to the most up-to-date version of the style guide

Vanessa manages the style guide with social media in mind. There's no reason to drop your brand when you have to reduce it to 140 characters (or fewer, if you want to get retweeted). That pressure can actually help you eliminate the noise that can otherwise distract from your core messages and message architecture itself.

"We're working to establish our themes for next year so we can start curating content for those topics," Vanessa continued. "That just makes our lives easier; we can prioritize new publications to time the release to tie in with the theme. We're not drafting new content every month; we're helping our users get to the existing content—content we actually already have—that's relevant to that theme."

AdoptUSKids is a world away from MINI, but embraces social media with a similar spirit of consistency, pragmatism, and investment—even if the overall budget is much smaller. Vanessa's colleague Pat Rhoades actually uses the metaphor of a car to describe how social media fits with their editorial processes and overall content strategy. "Our social media is just a wheel on the car," Vanessa concluded. "It's not the car itself, it's not driving the car, but that wheel needs to spin in tandem with every other type of communication we put out. Our editorial process is the roadmap, and the calendar? The calendar's the driver."

CHAPTER 8

GROWING THE BUSINESS AND GETTING TO WORK

GET A SEAT AT THE TABLE

"Content work can't be divorced from business goals, so content people need to know as much as possible about the client's understanding of their goals," writes Erin Kissane.[1] She recommends the content strategist dig deep into project documentation, the RFP, and proposal to forge a working, realistic project definition. If you are on the project in that capacity—whether you are The Content Strategist, a lone wolf wearing *all* the hats, or the Information Architect (IA) or copywriter who sees the communication gaps—grab a seat at the table and champion clarity. Even (and especially) in internal initiatives, the content strategist owes it to the budget, stakeholders, and team to clarify the business goals, communication goals, and overarching project objectives.

That's all good and necessary, but it can be absurdly difficult if you wait to incorporate a content strategy perspective until after the project has been scoped. In this chapter, let's address that from two perspectives:

- How to (and why to) pull a content strategist into the sales process early so as to affect the outcome of proposals and pitches and ensure the work you propose aligns with the objectives of the project
- How to use content strategy as a "wedge" service to open the door for more comprehensive follow-on work and complete engagements

You've made it this far. Now, how can you start *doing* this work, whether you're going to incorporate content strategy–related activities and deliverables into your own work, or advocate for a content strategist to join your team? If you're an agency account executive, there's stuff here for you, too. You probably already face the challenges of selling a variety of services and sussing out clients' needs—explicit and implicit—from what they *say* they need. (If you've spent any time in the trenches, you're familiar with the wide expanse between those two lists.) Content strategy can make your job easier. In this chapter, we'll spill secrets. I reached out to content strategists active around

---

[1] *The Elements of Content Strategy (A Book Apart, 2011).*

the world, in independent consultancies, freelance relationships, big agencies, and in-house creative teams, to learn how they sell (upsell, cross-sell, and "sneaky sell") their work.

USE CONTENT STRATEGY TO WIN

In my experience at digital interactive agencies large and small, content strategy is the offering that often sets the team apart and could help us win work. There are several ways you can flaunt your strategy savvy and position your team for similar results.

DEMONSTRATE COMMITMENT BEYOND THE CAMPAIGN OR LAUNCH

Companies that court agencies by "dating around" to find the special team to design their app or overhaul their web presence are pretty smart. They separate the "love 'em and leave 'em" agencies from the ones they could bring home to Mother. The former might just stick around for launch and then rush on to the next hot new gig, while the latter demonstrate their investment in a long-term relationship. You want to be in that group, and content strategy can help you stand out.

As we've discussed throughout this book, the content strategist doesn't just get involved at the beginning, or jump in for a phase and then leave, gallivanting off to the next engagement. No, they're in it for the long haul with tasks throughout the project:

- Clarify communication goals in the beginning
- Identify and organize content to manifest those goals
- Figure out how to get that content (and continue to get it at the right frequency and in a consistent format) throughout the life of the experience
- Ensure the content can thrive long after the rest of the team steps away from the stakeholders

In many large agencies, an individual resource can't always stick around throughout the whole project, but content strategy as a practice at least lays the groundwork for longer-term planning and execution. By including content strategy in the team, *and* explaining its role and involvement, you're indicating a commitment to governance, execution, and shared success. If you manage relationships with universities or count a number of large institutions among your accounts, you know this is the type of thing they appreciate.

In other cases, your prospective clients might not recognize the value of long-term content strategy—but that might be the very element of continuity and engagement the project needs to maintain communication and ensure its success. When you see it, and the rest of the team sees it—no doubt because they read the earlier chapters in this very book, right?—how can you help your client see it?

In some agencies, I know it can be tough to carve out a continuing budget for this kind of involvement. Not for explicit deliverables ("how many hours do you need for each iteration of landing page content?") but rather just for continued *involvement*: oversight, mentoring calls, "office hours," and drop-in labs like we discussed in Chapter 6. Your agency might prefer something that looks less like maintenance and more like additional, more targeted project work. Your prospective client may be warming to content strategy, but may still not be on board for this kind of long-term relationship.

Here's how I like to get past that when I'm talking with a prospective client or a new client and we're feeling out the right budget for the scope:

> "We've found that at specific points in this type of work, people can lose momentum or depart from the central vision. Given the investment you're making and our past experience, we recommend building in time at those 'pressure points' to ensure *the continued successful application* of the content strategy as you execute it."

I've found most prospective clients don't balk at this approach. If they do, there might be a bigger issue I need to address:

- They don't yet fully understand the value proposition of content strategy—so I need to educate them before they enter into a financial commitment.
- They're looking for a quick tactical job, not a strategic relationship comprising continued involvement or small projects—so I need to help them see why a quick fix won't solve their long-term challenges. Or, I need to refer their business elsewhere.
- They just don't have the budget to address the full scope with this level of engagement and oversight.

This applies whether you're selling a new website, CMS evaluation and integration, social media strategy, or application engineering: if you're helping a team wrangle content, don't leave them hanging.

In the third case, there's a terrific opportunity—and if you're an account executive, this is big for you. In projects of limited budget (you know, like *every* project), ethical consulting demands we match the scope of work to the depth of engagement.

Let's say you're proposing a $75,000 engagement to overhaul an ecommerce website. You can divvy up the budget for a scope that favors depth or breadth. If you favor breadth, the more common tendency, the IA might wireframe pages in every section of the site and the content strategist might conduct a full audit of the current site.

But what happens if you favor depth of engagement? In that case, the content strategist will need to get creative. Rather than conducting a comprehensive audit, she might only audit the top three levels of content across the site, and choose just one vertical to "core sample" in detail—and then extrapolate from there. Or, your content strategist might create a template for the audit, and then he might share it with the main content manager on the client side so that that person can audit their own content. In that model, the content strategist will spend more time training and periodically checking in with the client's content manager, but that relationship will allow the client to gain greater knowledge of the content they will ultimately own. As the content strategist teaches your client to fish, they'll get into a pattern of frequent checkpoints and mentoring—communication that can fuel the success of the project and possibly facilitate other opportunities.

Pull your content strategist close to help you and your prospective client figure this out in the proposal process. They'll take into account company culture and evaluate the client's skill levels and familiarity with the subject matter. Together, you'll "right-size" the project to allocate time to the level of hand-holding the client needs in order to love your work and succeed in their efforts—regardless of the budget. Relly Annett-Baker of Supernice Studio puts this into perspective: "No one would add 'develop site' to the list of requirements without talking to a developer."[2] So while content strategy is also not just a phase or deliverable, make sure you consult with a content strategist to define content strategy and the communication around it in your list of requirements.

DEMONSTRATE YOU HAVE A COMPREHENSIVE OFFERING THAT ADDRESSES WHY PEOPLE USE THE WEB

As we discussed, content strategy can fuel the communication necessary for a long-term commitment to user experience. On a slightly more tactical level, by offering content strategy as part of your team and approach, you're also showing prospective clients that your team can address all the facets of user experience design: structural, aesthetic, and substantive. Complementing information architecture and visual design, content strategy is the third part of the trinity

---

[2] "Love Thy Geek: Working In and Amongst Web Teams," Confab 2011, http://www.slideshare.net/RellyAB/love-thy-geek-working-in-and-amongst-web-teams.

of skills—the third leg in the stool—to prescribe a front-end design.[3] This is a comprehensive offering that demonstrates your team understands why people use the web, download an app, or socialize online: they do it for the content.

The web is made of content, and by including content strategy in proposed solutions, you're telling prospective clients that your team has the maturity and wisdom to meet the needs of their customers—even if those clients don't yet understand them.

Many organizations are savvy enough to their own needs that they request help with content strategy by name. But just a few years ago, that wasn't the case, and it still isn't always the case even when it would clearly strengthen the work of the rest of the team, ensure the long-term success of the initiative, and likely enhance the post-project relationship so as to drive additional work. Consider some of the requests your prospects might bring to the table—and how and why to bring content strategy into your response:

Prospective client wants ...	Your response should include ...	Why?
■ New look-and-feel! Just a reskinning! See also: website redesign	■ Content strategy including message architecture and editorial style guidelines	■ If they want to look different— to flaunt change, respond to competitor rebranding, etc.— they need to sound different too.
■ Homepage and landing page copy or copyediting	■ Content strategy including message architecture and editorial style guidelines	■ If they want new content, you need to know the goals and standards to which to write or edit it.
■ CMS implementation	■ Content strategy including content audit and content model with training and mentoring and exploration of governance	■ Before they "just port over the existing content," they need to know if the new system will support it and the culture creating it. An audit can also identify content to leave behind—saving time and money.
■ Social media strategy/training/ ghostwriting	■ Content strategy including message architecture, editorial style guidelines, editorial calendar, training	■ Before they embark on engagement, they deserve clear goals, direction, and planning— otherwise, they will sound like one of the other million aimless organizations on the Internet. Save them from themselves.

In these examples, I've recommended a response that includes specific deliverables more than the broader processes. This is a starting point. Work with your content strategist to figure out the context and frequency of communication; deliverables are just milestones in the conversation and, for better or worse, the common currency of most consulting engagements.

---

[3] Of course, the stool might be solid but wholly inappropriate without the inputs of user research. And it might only be an unrealized vision without the backend magic of skilled developers. And no one might ever sit on it, were it not for social media and search engine optimization! And it might never evolve, without the constant vigilance of a measurement and analytics team! But c'mon ... get your own metaphor.

See the needs that a client may bring to the table? Those all demand content strategy—they just don't always ask for it by name. Of course, it's not always easy to have this conversation. Your prospective client asks for the shiny object, the sweet dessert, and you need to be a strict but empathetic parent.

Yes, they can have the cookies, but they need to eat some vegetables first.

So, you help them see the value in the vegetables. And your prospective client isn't a petulant three-year-old, so hopefully, you can make your case. Because in the long run, it will just be better for them. Content strategy that drives their website design is *better for them*, if they hope to maintain an engaging web presence over time that meets the needs of their audience and organization. Whether you're in an outside consultancy or an in-house marketing department, your clients are turning to you for your wisdom: you've learned from experience they don't have. It doesn't hurt to subtly and respectfully remind them of that so that you can continue to set yourself up for success on their project and do the work well, not just do work.

Help them embrace content as an asset

An organization may issue an RFP because they need to improve their standing in the marketplace through their marketing, especially their web presence. For many organizations, content is a differentiator—and good content may just be *their* differentiator if their competitors fail to create, maintain, curate, or organize it well. In Chapter 5, we discussed how Bows-n-Ties.com does this to stand out for both search engines and curious customers. In Chapter 3, we discussed how REALTOR.org engages in similar work. Not only do they cull their content for historical value, staff librarians also constantly evaluate, curate, and republish their content and cutting-edge original research. This serves dual goals:

- Content informs and empowers their primary audience, helping them do their jobs better
- Well-curated content positions their site and organization as the pre-eminent thought leader in the industry

Sound familiar? You probably have many clients with similar aspirations of being the valuable, indispensable, go-to source for information, quotes, and forecasting in their industry. With an appropriate content strategy, content might be the very thing to help them achieve these goals.

That's exactly how it plays out for REALTOR.org. As we discussed in Chapter 3, the site serves the National Association of Realtors® by publishing content on the array of topics real estate professionals encounter. Frederik Heller, the manager of the NAR's Virtual Library and Archives, explained how content has long been the organization's primary value and product.[4]

"The National Association of Realtors was founded in 1908 as the industry was getting off the ground," he began. "Our organization was formed to pull together the different interests and start promoting educational standards and offer information on appraising, marketing, and the business of real estate brokerage." They formed an internal library in 1923. "It's here to educate members and act as a resource."

"In the '90's, they asked us to consolidate departments and get more efficient in the control and distribution of information; we formed Information Central," added John Krukoff, the director of that group. Now, there are 17 people who act as information specialists, including seven librarians, all in the service of maintaining and disseminating content. Mary Martinez-Garcia is NAR's library manager and chief librarian. She manages research for staff, academics, and members.

"As far as the creating web content, managing web content, and acquiring content, our librarians are out there, on the forefront, training our members," she explained. "We're involved in projects in the association to keep the organization's information accessible and preserved."

What's the value in all that? Why does it matter? "NAR was founded as the industry was getting off the ground, so part of NAR's history is the history of housing laws and real estate in the country," Frederik noted. "Annual conventions, size of membership, things that happened during the Depression . . . we're not just sentimental, looking back, but also analyzing similar situations in history to see how they were handled. NAR has been actively involved in shaping federal and state housing policies. Our lobbyists look back at those discussions to influence their efforts in Washington now." NAR's own lobbyists can use this information, but so can policy makers and the media. REALTOR.org offers content that helps the organization, academics, and the media understand political issues and affect legislation. Their content is unique in its breadth and focus for aiding these conversations. One of the ways the organization curates its content helps manifest this value and cultivate information from deep in the archives.

The *quintessential reference*—what company wouldn't want to claim that about their content? Isn't this the accolade REI is working toward with its "expert advice" and printed guides?

"Librarians often create Pathfinders," John explained. "Our Pathfinders morphed into Field Guides, 130 some or so that are managed within our group, accessed by all sorts of organizations or groups. They've become the quintessential reference for anything in real estate."

[4] Heller, F., Krukoff, J., and Martinez-Garcia, M. (24 February 2011). Personal interview.

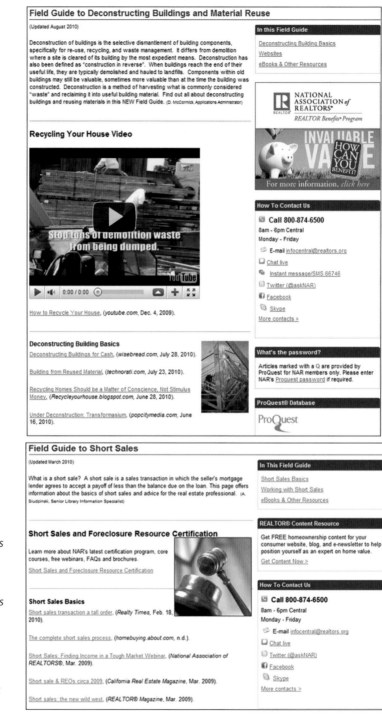

Field guides cover a broad range of topics. Here, guides to building material reuse and short sales offer Realtors original content, links to other sources, links to recent articles, links to educational websites, video, and REALTOR.org's own ebooks. NAR is the single best source of this information for the target audience.

"They provide a central point for anyone to find information related to real estate—how to market with Twitter, how to open a brokerage, etc.," Frederik continued. "We provide links to ebooks, links to recent articles, summaries of websites. It's meant to be a one-stop place where Realtors can find this information quickly. The ideas for topics come from several places. Some come from Realtors; they can email ideas for topics, and we also get calls for questions about a certain topic. We'll try to identify trends. Sometimes other staff members raise issues and suggest we need a field guide. We also monitor news and industry press for when trends come up." Because the librarians staff NAR's customer service lines, they're able to keep a finger on the pulse of hot topics and needs within their target audience.

USE CONTENT STRATEGY AS A WEDGE

We've discussed how content strategy can open the door to a long-term relationship with your client, and how it allows you to audit and promote the content that may very well be your client's biggest asset. Content strategy can also help you, as an account manager, more realistically scope projects and lay the groundwork for larger engagements. (This is true whether you're working with an external client or putting together the budget for an internal initiative.) Let's discuss how you can use content strategy—or elements of the practice—as a wedge service to open the door for more comprehensive engagements.

START BY LISTENING TO THE ISSUES

"Often, clients will describe the framework of what's going on," explained Ahava Leibtag, the content strategist we met in Chapter 3.[5] "They know where the holes are, but they often have no idea how to move things to get what they want." Prospects might be confronting migration malaise, frustration with obsolete content, or ineffective publishing workflow. She listens, taking an approach that's not native to content strategy: *consultative selling* is the process in which an account manager or salesperson helps a prospective client articulate the problem or need, rather than just pitching a solution.

"What I do is offer a *piece* of content strategy," she continued. "Typically a content audit if they're concerned about migration . . . [it's] a tangible deliverable, and people will often pay for that. Recently, a major institution was getting ready to move a detailed legacy site over to their main platform. It had taken more than two years to convince the site owner to move the site, and the web team was very concerned about how to go about doing this. I did a very

In some corporate cultures, you can roll an audit into a small paid engagement to suss out the nature of the bigger project. This has value to both the client and the agency or individual considering the work, so it's not inappropriate to charge for it.

[5] Leibtag, A. (1 August 2011). Personal interview.

thorough content audit for them with a detailed site map, and they absolutely loved it. It gave them so much information that wasn't sitting on the surface, so they felt very confident to move ahead with hiring me," she concluded.

In Chapter 3, we discussed the differences between quantitative and qualitative content audits; here, Ahava is describing a *quantitative* audit. It works as a stand-alone piece to open the door to dig deeper into the content—and the client organization itself. I often approach this type of work by conducting a quantitative audit with the understanding that after I know more about the client and their goals, we'll document those goals in a message architecture. That, in turn, becomes the yardstick against which we can conduct a *qualitative* content audit.

Ahava works as an independent consultant, not in the context of a multifaceted team or agency, so you can see how this approach works for the lone wolf consultant as well. If that's you, you know what it's like to wear the many hats of specialist, salesperson, project manager, and bookkeeper; creative approaches to streamline the sales process never hurt, right?

CONDUCT A HIGH-LEVEL AUDIT TO INFORM SCOPE WITH GREATER REALITY

Another use for a content audit is to help your own scoping process. We previously discussed the quick-and-dirty approach of conducting a more minimal audit to save budget and allow for investment in other areas. This is a similar practice.

Regardless of its size or depth, you'll never conduct a content audit for its own sake; rather, your content strategist will do it to learn more about what they're confronting, determine the quality of current content, or help the information architecture understand the breadth of content types. In the pre-sales process, a content strategist can conduct a more superficial or incomplete content audit and extrapolate. You'll gain several pieces of information from this process:

- A better sense of how long it will take to conduct a full content audit
- An accurate assessment of the number of pages, screens, or modules in the prospective project
- High-level understanding of the range of content types
- A first blush grasp of the quality and redundancy of existing content

The "some information is better than no information" approach is something you should apply before committing to any big job, like helping a friend move or volunteering to clean out the fridge. It might just take longer and require more bleach than you think.

None of this is precise, complete, or final, and it would be arrogant and presumptuous to think it is—but it is useful scouting. And even *some* information is better than having *no* information about the mess you're proposing to fix.

Diana Railton, director of DRCC, a corporate communications agency in the UK, employs this approach. "We regularly carry out 'core samples' of a few sections of a site and use these to illustrate, in a more detailed proposal, the problems that needs addressing," she began.[6] This allows them to upsell more comprehensive content strategy to clients that may have only considered copywriting.

"A lot of our content strategy consultancy starts when organizations ask for training on web writing. Finding out what they're up against opens a whole Pandora's Box, as you can imagine," she added. An audit may reveal inconsistent messaging, multiple styles, fractured cross-channel experiences, and orphaned sections that demand sustainable plans for editorial workflow, not just better copy. Comprehensive content strategy that begins with communication goals and includes planning for creation, aggregation, organization, and governance can address all those issues.

Halfway across the globe in Brisbane, Australia, Sally Bagshaw describes a similar approach. At this writing, Sally is a freelance copywriter and content strategist, but spent much of the last decade as a web project manager with the Queensland Government and content team manager with the Department of Education.

"When I was working in-house as part of a web team, we'd use content audits as a tool to convince business areas that their sections of either the intranet or website needed some love.[7] Often business areas had no idea of the volume of content that was live and neglected," she noted.[8]

"That's the beauty of a spreadsheet," she added. "Content owners or subject matter experts aren't necessarily web savvy; asking them to review a section of a website without some guidance is usually an exercise in futility." That's why your prospective client may approach you for a website redesign or custom blogging platform and fail to ask for help with their content: they're just too close to it. But consider everything we've discussed so far: content strategy can help an organization communicate effectively, consistently, and sustainably. It's your job, and ethical obligation, not to just deliver what they ask, but to help them realize what they need.

---

[6] Railton, D. (1 August 2011). Personal interview.
[7] This applies to social media and other channels as well.
[8] Bagshaw, S. (1 August 2011). Personal interview.

"The beauty of a spreadsheet is that it translates an abstract concept (how content works on a site) into something quite tangible. No one can ignore endless rows of content marked as 'out of date.'" Spreadsheets, like mosquito bites, are nearly impossible to ignore. "It's a good tool to inspire (or provoke) action... especially if you're an internal person trying to do good but don't have the support to do it."

STOP READING AND GET TO WORK

Sally hits on a key point, whether you're in an agency team and feel like your client isn't hearing you or if you're in an internal team and getting lost in the shuffle of conflicting priorities: a content audit amplifies the problem. As most organizations favor resolution and order over entropy, problems demand solutions. And you can charge for that.

Of course, this is bigger than just the purpose and role of a content audit. In many projects, this is the purpose and role of a content strategist. We point out the emperor's clothing calamity. We encourage others who might prefer to ignore the situation to recognize it as a problem, invest time and money and effort in addressing it, and then determine how we're going to get suitable attire for seasons to come. This is the challenge of content strategy—and now it's your challenge too.

The goal is to engage in a project or process that will result in a better user experience, one that transcends channel, campaign, or budget cycle. The goal is to establish a sustainable publishing model for your clients and their customers. The goal is to facilitate better, more useful communication, and that cannot happen without content strategy.

This is a daunting challenge, but our users, clients, customers, and readers deserve no less than our bravery.

Fortune favors the bold. Ready?

INDEX

Note: Page numbers followed by *b* indicate boxes; *f* figures; *t* tables; *np* footnotes.

Check out our extensive list of titles in the area of UX/ HCI